Harry Allen has taught in Donaghadee since 1961 and lived in the town since the mid-1970s with his wife Valerie and family. One son, Jeffrey, and another son, Billy, and his wife Kathryn, also live in the town. Harry has been collecting documents about Donaghadee and the surrounding district for over thirty years, completing an Open University degree course in historical research methods to aid his investigations. His first book, The Men of the Ards, *appeared in 2004.*

To Olga,
Harry Allen
7th November 2006

This book has been sponsored by:

Muir
Higginson

Ards Borough Council

William Montgomery & Nicholas Day

DONAGHADEE
an illustrated history

Harry Allen

The White Row Press

DONAGHADEE

an illustrated history

Harry Allen

WHITE ROW

The White Row Press

First published 2006 by
The White Row Press
135 Cumberland Road
Dundonald, Belfast BT16 2BB
Northern Ireland

View our books at: www.whiterowpress.com

Cover: 'View of Donaghadee from the South Quay', 1832,
by D. Kennedy, reproduced with the permission of Joan Boyd.

This book has been financially supported by Ards Borough Council via the Donaghadee
Regeneration Group, Nicholas Day & William Mongomery, Gordons Chemists, Muir
Higginson, and Pier 36. The publishers extend their grateful thanks to these sponsors and
salute the civic spirit of all concerned.

ISBN (current) 1 870132 31 9
ISBN (new) 978 1 870132 31 2

Printed by the Universities Press Ltd., Belfast
A catalogue record for this book is available from the British Library

Contents

Preface

Every town or village has its story, and this can often have its place in 'big history'. What follows is my version of Donaghadee's story. It is no more than that. I have not tried to be definitive or comprehensive. While this work has been written for the general reader, I have also tried to point the serious student towards sources that contain additional detail and are perhaps worth further study.

2006 is a special year for Donaghadee. It is the 400th anniversary of what many would argue is the single most significant date in its history, the Ulster-Scots Plantation. If a certain Hugh Montgomery's ambitions had been denied in 1606, or diverted elsewhere, there might not have been much of a history of Donaghadee to write.

Donaghadee went on to become 'the gateway to Ulster', a place that in its time was as nationally famous as Dover or Holyhead, a fact that has been all but forgotten. This book observes, explains, and where appropriate, celebrates its rise.

It would be remiss indeed if I did not here record my sincere gratitude to the staffs, past and present, of the Public Record Office of Northern Ireland, the Queen's University Library and Teachers' Centre, the Linenhall Library, the National Library of Ireland, the National Archives of Ireland, Donaghadee Branch Library and other libraries of the South Eastern Education and Library Board for their help over the years. I am also indebted to Bill Crawford for his always generous help and advice, and, along with John Caldwell, for reading the early manuscripts and offering some helpful suggestions.

I would also like to thank Tom Neill for the use of his photographs of his great-great-grandmother Grace Neill, and for some interesting information about her close relatives; Cailean McClean of the Isle of Skye for his Hebridean viewpoint on 'The ship of the people'; my one-time Open University tutor Brenda Collins for her help with the complicated story of Ulster embroidery, the late Mrs Georgina Stone for some Delacherois information, pictures etc., and of course the book's select band of sponsors, whose ready support for this project gives me confidence in the future of the town.

Many Donaghadee people like Arthur Arbuckle, Fergus Bell, David Capper, Jean Cowan, Angélique Day, Pauline Drennan, Billy Hamilton, Betty Henry, Ralph & Jean Lock, Hugh Nelson, Billy Pollock, Willie Roberts, the late John Bennett and others, have been most generous with their suggestions and information over many years.

My wife Valerie has always supported my interest in local history. In recent months she has also become an assiduous proof-reader, and has even allowed me some of 'her' time on the family computer to put much of the work together. I could not have completed this work without her forbearance and understanding.

I would like to dedicate this book to my two sons, Jeff and Bill, for reasons only they know.

Finally, I would like to express my gratitude to Peter Carr of White Row Press who commissioned this history, and whose constant support and strict editing has helped me to express my thoughts more concisely. Thank you all for your help. Any errors or misconceptions that are contained in these pages are my own.

Harry Allen
Donaghadee, September 2006

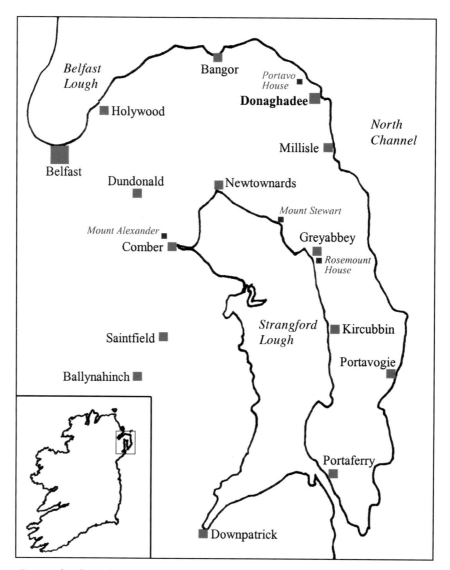

Belfast Lough

Bangor

Portavo House

Donaghadee

Holywood

North Channel

Millisle

Belfast

Dundonald

Newtownards

Mount Stewart

Mount Alexander

Greyabbey

Comber

Rosemount House

Strangford Lough

Kircubbin

Saintfield

Portavogie

Ballynahinch

Portaferry

Downpatrick

Donaghadee, County Down, and environs.

1 Early days

A watery birth

The small, picturesque town of Donaghadee lies near the head of the Ards peninsula in County Down. To the west, lies the drumlin landscape for which County Down is justly famous. To the east lies the Irish Sea, and just twenty miles off, Scotland, just two hours away by sail, and clearly and tantalisingly visible on a good day.

Donaghadee harbour, 1995. (Andrew J. Crawford)

Petrified firework display. When this unprepossessing pebble was split by the author in the summer of 2005, numerous almost perfectly preserved graptolites were found inside.

We are used to thinking of Donaghadee as a seaside town. Around 410-420 million years ago, however, when the Silurian rocks that underlie the town were formed, 'Donaghadee' lay not beside the chilly waters of the Irish Sea but deep beneath a warm, clear, tropical ocean.

The skeletons of the tiny creatures that lived in this ocean – the oldest organisms known from Ireland – can be found in profusion in Donaghadee. They are known as graptolites, and countless number of their remains can be found in the geologically renowned graptolite 'graveyard' of Coalpit Bay beside the Commons. Were the lifespan of the earth to be likened to a twenty four hour day, these little creatures did not appear until just after 9.30 pm, which is not late when we consider that, on the same scale, mankind arrived at less than one minute to midnight.

When the graptolites died, their tiny shell-like skeletons fell to the ocean floor to be covered by mud that would eventually become rock.[1] As their fossils show, graptolites were tiny, usually less than an inch in length. They can be found in

Coalpit Bay's [2] coastal mudstones, but are more easily discovered in the almost-black, flattish pebbles that litter its foreshore. Give the pebbles a couple of cracks on their edges, and they sometimes (but not always!) split along their strata to disclose these hidden treasures. Graptolites come in many varieties. They are often described as looking like fine pencil markings, many looking uncannily like watch-springs, and, once seen, are unmistakable.

Early settlement
Man arrived in Ireland following the end of the last Ice Age, some 10,000 years ago. Sea levels were lower, and it is not known where the first settlers landed, but it is tempting to think that Donaghadee might have been a 'gateway to Ireland' even then, and that some, taking advantage of the short sea passage from Galloway, may have landed near the site of the present town and begun new lives there.

These first Irish people lived by fishing, hunting wild animals, and gathering fruits, nuts, roots and berries. Around six thousand years ago, these hunter-

Donaghadee's Norman motte, viewed here circa.1930, is one of most splendid in Ulster. Archaeologists believe it that occupies the site of an even older rath or ringfort. (Robert Neill Collection)

The Moat, Donaghadee.

gatherers were displaced by new settlers, who domesticated animals and planted their own simple crops. Wave after wave of settlers, or more probably invaders, followed. 'Beaker people', bronze workers, Cruthnic peoples, Celts, Vikings, and Normans all made their mark here, in their day.

Needless to say, few traces of these ancient cultures remain. Some Neolithic flints have been found inland from Donaghadee, and the fine standing stone at Portavo may be the last remnant of a Neolithic burial monument.[3] Bronze Age bowls have been discovered at Ballywilliam and Ballyvester. Bronze Age axes have been found in 'Donaghadee' and the Cottown; which has also yielded a bronze cauldron, used for entertaining.[4]

Remains from the first century AD have also been found. In 1851, a grave containing beads, blue glass armlets and bronzes was dug up in Killaughey.[5] These grave goods are intriguing because they are Roman, or Roman influenced. They belonged to a woman of wealth and standing, and originated in the south of England. Their presence could be seen as pointing up the importance of Donaghadee as a port as far back as Roman times.

Raths from the Early Medieval period are scattered widely across Donaghadee's hinterland. Its greatest earthen monument, however, is its fine Norman motte, which was probably erected in John de Courcy's time (c.1180) to guard the port. Donaghadee boasts one of the largest mottes in Ulster. On a clear day, one can see the Copeland Islands, County Antrim, Galloway, Scafell Pike, the Isle of Man, and the Mourne Mountains from its summit. Its almost grandiose scale suggests that the port then had enormous strategic importance.

Although Donaghadee is mentioned in medieval records, the origins of its name are obscure. In the 1830s, John O'Donovan believed that the name might derive from *Domhnach dith,* the 'church of the loss', or *Domhnach Dioghbhalach,* meaning 'hurtful Sunday'. Recent researchers have favoured the rather less evocative *Domhnach Daoi* or 'Daoi's church'.[6]

By the mid-sixteenth century, the Norman settlement had collapsed, and Donaghadee lay within the territory of the O'Neills of Clandeboye. Though the O'Neills repeatedly declared themselves to be loyal subjects, Queen Elizabeth nonetheless granted her Secretary of State, Sir Thomas Smith, leave to found a colony in 'the Ardes... a rich and pleasant country on the eastern coast of Ulster.' Smith's son came to conquer and settle the Ards so that its 'half-barbarous people might be taught some civility.'[7] This wretched and embarrassing undertaking collapsed in 1573.

In the 1590s, after decades of provocation, Gaelic Ulster rose against the

Style-conscious Irish footsoldier of c.1590. Note his fashionable long fringe or 'glib'.

crown. A bitter war of attrition followed. In 1603 the Irish were forced to sue for peace. The power of Ulster's great Gaelic lordships had been broken, and the stage was set for radical social and political change, change that would lead to the birth of the modern town of Donaghadee.

The beginnings of modern Donaghadee

1603 found Con O'Neill, the Gaelic lord of South Clandeboye, languishing in a Carrickfergus dungeon, charged with waging war against the Queen. When word of his plight, and the fact that he held 60,000 acres, reached Hugh Montgomery, the sixth Laird of Braidstane in Ayrshire, Montgomery immediately hatched a devious plan. He employed an agent to woo the female gaoler at the Castle, allowing him to free the Irish chieftain. He then convinced O'Neill that he could get him a royal pardon. All Montgomery asked in return was title to half of O'Neill's vast estate.

At this point two other Ayrshire men enter the story, Sir James Fullerton and Sir James Hamilton, the latter described as 'once a schoolmaster, tho' afterwards made a person of honour.'[8] Both men had taught in Fullerton's school in Dublin. However, a career in education had never held any great appeal for either, and in time both gave up teaching in favour of performing covert services for James VI of Scotland, rising to become Privy Councillors in James's English court.[9]

Hamilton knew of O'Neill's difficulties and confided to Fullerton that he too had ambitions to gain the Clandeboye lands. Between them they persuaded the King that it would be better to divide South Clandeboye into three lots, i.e. between O'Neill, Hamilton and Montgomery. This, they claimed, would allow them to turn a troublesome wasteland into a productive colony. The scheme obtained royal approval in April 1605. Hamilton acquired lands along the north coast of Down and around Killyleagh. Montgomery received the Great Ardes and the ancient town of Blathewyc (Newtownards), which in 1605 is said to have comprised little more than a ruined priory and the stump of its old castle.

Aware that if he could not resettle his new lands, his grant would mean nothing, Montgomery began organising the migration of Presbyterians from lowland Scotland into County Down. The point of entry for most of these settlers was the port of Donaghadee. When Montgomery and his men arrived, they assembled on its undeveloped foreshore, then made their hesitant way round the great Gransha or Cottown Bog to Newtownards.

Some forty years later, Montgomery's grandson recalled that the parishes of

James Hamilton, c.1628. Unfortunately no likeness of his bitter rival Hugh Montgomery, the owner of Donaghadee, has survived. (National Trust)

Donaghadee, Greyabbey and Newtownards were:

more wasted than America when the Spaniards landed there... In all those three parishes aforesaid, 30 cabins could not be found, nor any stone walls, but ruined roofless churches, and a few vaults at Greyabbey, and a stump of an old castle in Newton, in each of which some Gentlemen sheltered themselves at their first coming over.[10]

Montgomery landed in Ulster 'in the springtime of 1606.' The year after his arrival, the first British colony was established in the Americas, at Jamestown in South Virginia.[11] Had one of these Virginia pioneers visited Montgomery's Ards he would have noted strong parallels between both endeavours. Climate and distance were very different of course, but both groups were seeking to establish a permanent settlement in an alien environment, and in the face of a wary native population.

A few of the colonists decided to settle in Donaghadee, whilst others filled the surrounding countryside. The settlers built homesteads and gradually enclosed the pastoral, Gaelic landscape. The native Irish remained, but were reduced to the status of 'Gibeonets and Garrons' who laboured or hewed timber.[12]

There were English in the new settlements, but it was mainly the Scots who made them flourish. Pynnar's 1619 survey reported that the Irish did not plough at all and the English ploughed very little, and that, 'Were it not for the Scottish tenants, who do plough... those parts may starve.'[13] Trade with the auld country grew. Montgomery's grandson recalled:

honest old men say that in June, July and August, 1607, people came from Stranraer, four miles, and left their horses at the port, hired horses at Donaghadee, came with their wares and provisions to Newton, and sold them, dined there, staid two or three hours, and returned to their houses the same day by bed-time, their land journey but 20 miles.[14]

However, not everyone who came to Ulster was industrious and God-fearing. In 1614 King James informed Ireland's new Lord Deputy that he had heard stories of cargoes being stolen near Donaghadee, and of shippers, 'bringing in idle, leiwd and disloyal persons whoe decline the Justice of the kingdome where they lived & trouble the plantation in these partes.'[15] One of Donaghadee's first Presbyterian ministers put it more baldly still:

From Scotland came many, and from England not a few, yet all of them the scum of

A north Down des. res.? The native Irish lived alongside the planters in traditional cabins such as these drawn by Thomas Raven in 1625-26. (North Down Heritage Centre)

both nations… fleeing from justice, or seeking shelter. In a few years there flocked such a multitude of people from Scotland that these northern counties of Down, Antrim, Londonderry etc. were in a good measure planted which had been waste before.[16]

In 1616, another observer described north Down as being populated with Scots, who 'do nothing for ornament or beautifying the country.'[17] This is fair comment. The settlers were still concerned with the business of survival. They laid out roads, erected churches and schools, planted hedges, encouraged the import of livestock, and generated trade. They had an excellent harvest in that first year of 1606, and thanks to their diligence in digging the ground, manuring it, and planting cereal crops and vegetables, the harvests improved in subsequent years. A water-mill was built in every parish.[18] The prosperity of farm holdings was such that rents rose at the rate of about ten per cent a year.[19]

Montgomery chose Newtownards as his administrative centre, and within five years the Plantation Commissioners recorded that:

Sir Hughe Montgomery knight hath repayred parte of the Abbey of Newtowne for his owne dwelling, and made a good towne of a hundred houses or thereaboutes all peopled with Scottes.[20]

For many years the 'towne' of Donaghadee would have been home to less than eight hundred people. If we think of a circle, half in the sea and half on land, with a diameter not much greater than about two hundred yards, Montgomery's little seaport town would easily have been enclosed inside the landward semicircle. It would have had about twenty to fifty houses along Sandy Row (the Parade and Shore Street), as many again up Back Street (Manor Street), Bow Street and the smaller lanes, with a semi-rural Manor House overlooking the 'towne' from what is now the Millisle Road.

The Plantation Commissioners recorded that James Hamilton, 'hath builded a fayre stone house at the towne of Bangor… [it] consistes of 80 neowe houses all inhabited with Scotishmen and Englishmen.'[21] The success of these colonies, and others in Antrim and Donegal, is thought to have had a strong influence upon James I's decision to proceed with the Plantation of Ulster in 1610.

But there was one important respect in which Hamilton and Montgomery's colonies offered a less than shining example to the 'official' plantation. Hamilton and Montgomery did not behave as partners in a great enterprise. Just the opposite. The two men fell out, and became bitter rivals. An endless jockeying for advantage followed.

Contemporary caricature of an Ulster planter. Note the chicken, duck, and sausages!

Donaghadee became a pawn in the rivalry between the two grandees. By processes unknown, Montgomery managed to transfer the legal title to the town and port of Donaghadee from Hamilton to himself.[22] He achieved an even greater coup in 1608, when he exchanged some of his lands near Ballymena for lands of similar value around Portpatrick in Scotland.[23] Montgomery now owned both sides of what would soon become known as the Short Sea Passage – the only person ever to do so.

In 1613 Montgomery's town of Newtownards was awarded the status of borough and Montgomery became its provost, or mayor. The town received the right to send two representatives to the Irish Parliament in Dublin.[24] This made him a power to be reckoned with. But Montgomery was far from done. He then attempted to acquire a royal warrant for Donaghadee that would give his harbour the monopoly of trade between Scotland and Ulster.

A Commission was formed to inquire into which ports should receive the prized royal warrant. The Commissioners recognised that Donaghadee had 'don much service allreaddie in the plantation,' and that it had a 'competent number

Making one's mark. Date-stone from 43 High Street, Donaghadee (Bailie's estate agency). JD and JS were probably newly-weds. Nothing is known about their lives.

of civille men alreddie settled and dwelling there'.[25] In 1616, after careful examination of all possible alternatives, the Commissioners concluded that:

they finde Donaghdy to be the only fittest place, betweene the River of Strangford & the River of Knockfergus for the saftie of Boates, the good ease of Passage, and the abbilitie of the Towne for entertainment of Passengers; & that the passage cannot be supplied under the number of sixteene Passage Boates, of eight, or Ten Tunne apiece or thereabouts.[26]

This was a triumph for the unstoppably entrepreneurial Montgomery. But even better news followed, when Portpatrick was nominated as warrant port on the Scottish side of the North Channel:

Portpatrick, then known as Portmontgomery, was by a charter granted by James VI to Sir Hugh Montgomery erected into a port, with power to exact dues and tolls on the traffic, which consisted chiefly of cattle and passengers, and an occasional mail.[27]

Henceforth, all travel between the Ards and Galloway had to be carried on between these two ports. Montgomery was jubilant. The terms of the warrant also gave him the right to hold a fair every June, and a weekly market in perpetuity. Within a year Donaghadee harbour was being described as the 'most usuall and frequentit for passage between Scotland and Ulster.'[28]

The warrant specified the fares on the boats to Scotland. A foot passenger paid eight pence (three modern pence) for a single journey; a horse was two shillings (ten pence); a horse and carriage cost fifteen shillings in the summer and a staggering one pound sterling in winter.[29] (This was at a time when a quart of best ale cost a penny, and a workman's wage for a year was £3.[30]) Surprisingly, for a mainly passenger service, cattle were permitted as cargo on these ships. Each cow or ox was carried at a cost of one shilling and sixpence in summer and two shillings in winter.

The port's success added considerably to Montgomery's wealth. By 1626 he had built a better harbour at Donaghadee and improved the facilities at Portpatrick. He was undoubtedly pleased with his progress. Within a few years he had built a handsome Manor House overlooking Donaghadee harbour and in a blaze of self-aggrandisement changed the names of the two terminus towns to Montgomery and Port Montgomery.[31] But this vanity came to nothing. The new 'official' names did not catch on, and the towns continued to be known by their ancient denominations.

In 1637 the Surveyor General, Charles Moncke, examined harbours and smuggling in the north of Ireland. Moncke reported that in the half-year from

For nearly four hundred years this lintel ('chalked' for clarity) remained over the door to Donaghadee's almost-forgotten Pound, proudly asserting Montgomery's ownership of the town.

Lady Day,[32] £644 in duties was collected by George Hull, the 'Customer' of Donaghadee, against £930 gathered from Bangor, Holywood, Conn's Water and Garmoyle near Belfast. £644 is a respectable figure, but it suggests that the Galloway trade may have proved less lucrative than Montgomery had hoped. Moncke recommended that Donaghadee build a custom-house, a wharf and crane, desks, and a sealed barrel for customs dues.[33] By 1649 a grand custom-house had been built beside Kelly's Steps.[34]

Donaghadee also had the advantage of being a post town, with a weekly mail service.[35] This was efficiently managed, with the result that the Portpatrick-Donaghadee route became recognised as the most dependable service across the Irish Sea. This mail service was in some ways the plantation's lifeline, and its regularity suggests that, on the eve of great Gaelic Rising of 1641, the settlement was bedding in relatively well.

The Rising shook the Ulster plantation to its foundations. Many Scots fled to their native shores, but others in and around Donaghadee town stood fast. The small town mustered a militia of over 120 men under the command of a Colonel Hoome.[36] It is not certain, but these men must have been part of the joint force taken by the Second Viscount Montgomery and Lord Hamilton to help the garrison at Lisburn repulse a major attack by Sir Phelim O'Neill.

The Rising was crushed, but the settlement languished, for the Rising and the subsequent War of the Three Kingdoms all but halted immigration into Ulster. Donaghadee would have to wait until the 1690s for the flow of settlers to resume, and for its precarious prosperity to revive.

2 Men o' war and a slave ship

The road to the Boyne

Donaghadee Parish Churchyard is entered through an old, wrought-iron double gate, hung on two fine stone pillars, with a view of the church tower behind them. On the inner side of the left hand gatepost is an inscribed black stone. Though it is nearly three hundred years old, the writing on it is still legible and reads as follows:

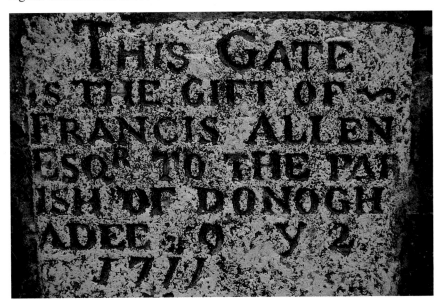

The 1711 church gate stone. Donaghadee's link with Schomberg and the tumultuous events of 1689.

Donaghadee's best-known homage to King Billy, crafted by Donaghadee builder and historian John Moore in the 1930s.

The original gate and gateposts were replaced long ago, but this gnarled stone has survived to excite our curiosity. Allen was clearly a man of substance, a man who did not wish to be forgotten. Who was this mysterious man?

The Delacherois Papers provide us with the answer. Amongst them is a statement of accounts prepared by one Francis Allen, agent of Hugh Montgomery, the Second Earl of Mount Alexander, and postmaster of Donaghadee.[1] The statement highlights Donaghadee's connection with one of the most significant conflicts in Irish history; for it is Mr Allen's claim for salary and expenses for work done in 1689 for the Duke of Schomberg, Commander-in-Chief of William III's forces in Ireland.

The general story is well known. After James II had fled to France, his daughter Mary and her husband William of Orange assumed the British throne as William III and Mary II. James, the legal monarch, then made it clear that, with the support of Louis XIV, he was determined to win back his throne.

The nation took sides. In the north of Ireland, a number of Ulster-Scots settlers met in Hillsborough to declare their support for King William. In March 1689, with Hugh Montgomery at their head, the Williamites marched south from Hillsborough to take on the Jacobites. They were roundly beaten at 'the Break of Dromore'.[2]

The word of this defeat, and of James's landing two days earlier at Kinsale, persuaded many of the Protestants of north Down to head for the safety of Londonderry. Others choked the roads leading to Donaghadee, seeking a passage to Portpatrick. There was pandemonium on the quayside because the packets and other boats could not cope with the hordes of refugees. As the numbers mounted the thoughts of many in Donaghadee turned from fear to anger and retaliation.

Before long these men chose a leader, an ex-army captain called Henry Hunter, who quickly forged a disciplined strike force out of local men and refugees. A determined campaign of resistance had begun.

Hearing that Newtown was being plundered, they immediately set out for the Strangford Lough shore, where they met the Jacobite force that had been sacking Newtownards. The two sides clashed at Cunningburn, where Hunter's ad hoc army amazed themselves by putting the larger Jacobite force to flight. Hunter immediately led his jubilant men to relieve a beleaguered Comber, and soon afterwards, Downpatrick.

But it was the Jacobites who held the initiative. In April, James marched north to Derry, whose people had been buoyed up by the uplifting stories from north Down. With both sides ready for a showdown, the siege of Derry began.

As the city lay under siege, William's naval forces under Major General Percy Kirke and Captain Sir George Rooke cruised the waters between the north of Ireland and Scotland in order to keep the sea clear of Jacobite ships.[3] Their base of operations was the little port of Donaghadee.[4] In June, Kirke led thirty vessels into Lough Foyle, and on July 30th 1689, under his direction, the *Mountjoy* broke the boom and relieved the siege after a gruelling 105 days.

Now the initiative passed to William. Since July 20th, the Duke of Schomberg had been anxiously waiting at the head of a great invasion force at the mouth of the Dee estuary. He needed a favourable wind to take his army to Ireland. And as McCarthy Mor's Jacobite forces held Carrickfergus, he also needed a good landing place on the safer northern shore of County Down.

It is at this point that Francis Allen enters the story. Most of the communication between Schomberg, Kirke, Rooke, and King William passed

Any letters today, Your Grace? Francis Allen handled the Duke of Schomberg's post in 1689.

through his small post office. On August 11th Schomberg's long awaited wind came, and the *Bonaventure* led his great fleet out of Hoylake.

By this point Captain Rooke's fleet had already anchored in 'Dunacade Bay' from which he reported that he had, 'got one small ship off. Four others we burn't, and broake about twenty boates.' These ruthless actions secured Schomberg a safe landing place in north Down.

The smoke of combat had hardly lifted when Rooke's lookouts reported the sails of Schomberg's ships hull down to the south-east. Rooke immediately stood out of Donaghadee Bay, ordered a ceremonial thirty-eight gun salute, and escorted the great fleet past the dangerous Briggs Rocks and into Bangor Bay. A week later the *London Gazette* reported:

From Bangor in the county of Downe in Ireland, August 13th, His Grace the Duke of Schomberg arrived this afternoon in this Bay. The forces are now landing.[5]

As James's forces were centred at Lisburn and Carrickfergus, the landing of men, munitions and stores at Bangor and Ballyholme went unopposed. The Jacobite position was now perilous. In Carrickfergus, McCarthy Mor would have heard Rooke's salute, and with a glass would have seen the sails of Schomberg's fleet. He burnt the town's suburbs, deployed his forces inside the castle, and prepared for Schomberg's onslaught.

The next day, Schomberg crossed the Lagan and invested Carrickfergus.[6] His warships bombarded the castle from the sea, and by August 27th 1689 Carrickfergus had fallen. Schomberg offered McCarthy Mor an honourable surrender, and he and his two thousand men marched from the castle, 'with Colours flying, Arms, and Drums beating.'[7]

Schomberg's humanity provoked a vitriolic reaction:

So rude were the Irish-Scots that the Duke was forced to ride in among them with his pistol in his hand to keep the Irish from being murdered. They striptd most part of the women and took it very ill that the Duke did not order them all to be put to death.[8]

Meantime, the waters off Donaghadee were alive with passing ships as reinforcements and supplies were hurried in. Schomberg then marched south to Dundalk, but his campaign was a disaster. Thanks to some overly cautious decisions, and an outbreak of typhus among his troops, Schomberg was forced to retreat, and the 1689 campaign fizzled to a close.

By the following June, William had landed at Carrickfergus, and James was marching north from Dublin. However the story of their meeting on the banks of the Boyne is a tale for another time.

Carrickfergus Castle c.1560. The castle would have looked much like this at the time of Schomberg's assault. (Irish Historic Towns Atlas)

What of Donaghadee's postmaster, Francis Allen? As the drama unfolded, Allen lived quietly in Ballynoe near Donaghadee, and spent his working hours carrying Schomberg's communications. In May 1690, just weeks before the Battle of the Boyne, anxious to be paid, Allen submitted his bill to the Postmaster-General. Its detail is fascinating. In late August 1689, for instance, we read that he claimed 9s 4d for riding to Carrickfergus on the 23rd to deliver a package addressed to Major General Kirke and Captain Rooke, and 19s 10d for twice 'waiting on his grace the Duke of Schomberge to Gett his grace's answer to a Packet from Scotland.'

Between September 12th and the end of November Allen claimed a further £5 4s 3d for the expense involved in sending five express packages to Schomberg and to Scotland.

He also claimed for the business he had conducted with the Donaghadee packets and other smaller boats. This added £15 to the tally. He then appended a claim for salary drafted, 'According to the Allowance given by the Lord Lieutenant and Council of Ireland on ye like occasions'. This amounted to another £21 5s 0d. The monies paid to his 'sub-postmaster', John Park, added an additional £15, making a grand total of £57 18s 2d.

There is no record of whether this impressive sum was ever paid, but one cannot imagine such a diligent man letting the matter slide. Comparisons of wages and prices between the seventeenth and twenty-first centuries are notoriously difficult, but Allen's claims, totalling almost £60, would certainly have made him a wealthy man in a very short time. No wonder he was able to spare a couple of pounds on a gate!

Donaghadee and the slave trade

On a November morning in 1739, the Newtownards Petty Constable rode into Donaghadee. He had come to investigate reports that a group of convicts had escaped from the town, and were at large somewhere in the Ards.

The Constable's arrival was followed by that of a bedraggled herd of men, women and children. Some were tied and shackled together. The Constable immediately stopped the group and questioned them. The man in charge of the prisoners was a certain William Davison, master of the *William*, a commercial vessel based in Donaghadee. He was accompanied by Norman McLeod, the twenty-four year old son of a Laird Donald McLeod of Berneray on the Isle of Skye, a close relation of the McLeod of McLeod, a clan chief in the Hebridean islands of Skye, Lewis and Harris. The drovers were crewmen from the *William*, and the shuffling wretches were their prisoners.

Davison told the Constable almost what he expected to hear. That the mariners had set out for Bangor in an attempt to recapture convicts who had escaped from sheds or barns in Donaghadee. That they had found them huddled in a Bangor ale-house and were returning them to custody.

It was a plausible story. And the prisoners were a grim looking bunch. Most were filthy. Some were bleeding. Others were limping and crying pitifully. None of them contradicted Davison. Indeed, none of them appeared to know any English.

But something about the story and the demeanour of the armed seamen aroused the Constable's suspicions. The timidity of some of the adult prisoners and the extreme youth of the children added to his unease. He refused to allow the prisoners to remain with Davison and McLeod, and took them back to the lock-up in Newtownards.

Within a few days at least thirty individuals were being held in Newtown, all supposedly escapees from the *William*. Who were the prisoners? What were their crimes? A court was hurriedly convened to get to the bottom of the matter.

Outhouse or gaol? According to local tradition, the Hebridean slaves were held in this barn (or its predecessor) at Herdstown House in 1739.

Two justices of the peace, William Montgomery of Rosemount and John Bailie of Kircubbin, sat on the bench.[9]

Because the prisoners could speak no English, the court had to rely mainly upon evidence supplied by the *William's* crew-members. One of these, Michael Murdogh of Donaghadee, was the first to testify. Four other crewmen followed. Their stories shocked the magistrates. Their tale was one of brutality, heartlessness and venality, and it was corroborated by two incriminating letters.[10] The crewmen claimed that they had been unwilling parties to events. That the villains of the peace had been Davison and McLeod.

Their story ran as follows. In the early summer of 1739, Norman McLeod and his father Donald had approached some sea captains in Donaghadee with an illegal, get-rich-quick scheme. Most of the captains had turned them down flat, but one man, one black sheep, William Davison, had taken up their offer.

McLeod's plan was simple. The *William* could carry about one hundred passengers if they were well jammed in. McLeod suggested taking a hundred people forcibly from their homes and selling them into slavery. They would not get their slaves from Africa. They would get them from the Hebrides, by

William Montgomery of Rosemount, JP, one of the compassionate magistrates who freed the forcibly imprisoned Scots. (Montgomery family)

whatever means proved necessary, then sail directly to Philadelphia in the New World where their passengers would work as indentured servants, in other words slaves. But how were they to obtain their cargo without arousing suspicion?

Norman McLeod had the answer. His kinsman, William McLeod, controlled a quasi-legal court that could 'convict' Davison's captives on spurious charges, giving the enterprise a cloak of legality. All would be sentenced to transportation.

The Donaghadee sailors gave heart-rending accounts of putting into small havens in Harris and Skye, and tricking men, women and children into boarding the *William*. Some of their victims were beaten and then carried semiconscious on to the boat, where they were held below decks, lying in their own filth. Some of the captives addressed the court in their native Gallic. Through an interpreter, one young woman told of being taken forcibly from her bed and then dragged by her ankles over the rocks, and then being hoisted on board, with no care shown for her person, and with nothing to cover her nakedness.

Donaghadee's customs collector at the time was a Ballyhay man called Luke St. Lawrence. He told the court in Newtownards how '12 or 13 of said persons not very fit for sale, six being under six years old, three big with children and a few very old' had been abandoned on the islands of Canna, Rum and Jura, as they were deemed to be more trouble than they were worth.[11]

This left McLeod and Davison with ninety-six men, women and children; enough, they decided, for a profitable trans-Atlantic crossing. Before commencing, Davison decided to re-victual his ship in his native Donaghadee.

And so the *William* tied up near Kelly's Steps. Davison ordered his 'convicts' to be stored in two large warehouses, one his own and one owned by a Francis McMinn of Herdstown House, a wealthy merchant who may have been the real owner of the *William*.[12] The seamen of the *William* may have been careless or possibly reluctant turnkeys, because a night or two later many of the prisoners escaped.

Hence the foray to Bangor, and the discovery of some of the escapees, who were driven back to Donaghadee with cudgels and iron bars. Others were subsequently recovered from bolt holes around the Ards. At the time of the hearing a number were still at large, as were Davison and McLeod.

The justices were satisfied that the so-called convicts had broken no laws. St. Lawrence emphasised that twenty of them were aged from six to ten years old and thus, 'by no law in any Christian country could be guilty of capital

House of shame? Herdstown House, the original McMinn homestead, still standing over 250 years later.

crimes.' The court had no hesitation in liberating the Hebrideans. However, this left the would-be slaves far from home, with no way of getting back there. Many stayed on, eventually finding work in the parish, and with luck, a life partner.[13]

Their harrowing story has been all but forgotten in Ireland, however it has not been forgotten in the west of Scotland. There, the saga of the *William* is remembered as *Soitheach nan daoine* or 'the ship of the people'.[14]

Hebridean historians see the story of the *William* as the tip of the iceberg. They see it as a horrifying glimpse into a secretive and almost wholly unrecorded trade that saw an unknown number of western Scots being forcibly shipped to North Carolina. There, plantation owners paid £5 for every poor soul who survived the Atlantic crossing.[15]

Luke St. Lawrence believed that Skye's clan chiefs had been behind the affair, and fumed to his fellow-collector at Portpatrick that McLeod and Davison deserved to hang if any court could find them guilty.[16] There is no record that any ever did.

3 The gateway to Ulster

Donaghadee's heyday

By the early eighteenth century, the plantation had become firmly established. Indeed it had become so well integrated with local society and so synonymous with it that it was no longer a thing apart.[1] As the plantation flourished, so did Donaghadee. In 1662 an improved mail service using an open boat was established between Donaghadee and Portpatrick with a grant of £200 per annum. In 1710 and 1755, Acts of Parliament ordered further improvements to the service.

In 1769, after years of criticism about the inadequacy of the facilities, the Packet Company, which owned the harbours at Donaghadee and Portpatrick, decided to invest in new harbours on both sides of the North Channel. John Smeaton, one of the leading marine architects of the day, was commissioned to build them. These fine new harbours were completed in 1774, at a cost of £10,000.[2]

The mail was then carried by the cutter *Buckingham,* and two fifty-five ton yachts, the *Hillsborough* and the *Charlotte*.[3] By 1791, three new fifty-ton vessels named the *Downshire*, the *Palmer* and the *Westmoreland* from Stalkartt's yard in Rotherhithe had joined the *Hillsborough* on the route. The speedy conveyance of the mails was such a priority that at least one of these vessels was obliged to be available at each port at all times, ready to sail for the other side as soon as it could after the arrival of a mail coach.

The only 'rival' Irish Sea service was from Dublin-Holyhead. All postal rates were calculated according to their distance from Donaghadee, Dublin and the Atlantic port of Waterford.[4] A measure of this is the surviving number of iron mileposts giving the distance from Dublin in Irish miles.[5] Until it fell into the sea in the 1990s, Donaghadee's proud equivalent stood on the Parade opposite Hunter's Lane, recording, 'Newtownards – 6, Belfast – 14, Dublin – 94 (Irish miles)'.

The mail or packet boats also carried passengers. Tickets for the journey could be obtained from packet agents, James Gillespie in Portpatrick and James Lemon in Donaghadee. In the two centuries since Montgomery's 1616 Warrant, the fares had roughly doubled, meaning that only the relatively wealthy could afford this form of transport.

The last decades of the eighteenth century undoubtedly constituted the heyday of the Donaghadee Packet Company, and the golden era of its hometown and port. Donaghadee was then a small town with a bustling port, widely known as the gateway to Ulster. Scarcely a day would have passed without a sighting on the quay of a person, sometimes with a grand entourage, whose name and importance had preceded them. The modern parallel would perhaps be Aldergrove, or the George Best Belfast City Airport.

Most Ulster landlords, from Lord Londonderry in the east to the Duke of Abercorn in the west, would regularly have made business and pleasure trips to Scotland and England. Indeed some were known to keep a *pied-à-terre* in Donaghadee, there to 'wait for a wind.'[6] The Earl of Abercorn, who owned coalfields near Edinburgh, had a more peremptory style. He once demanded that his banker, 'get a small full-decked ship hired to come over for me from Donaghadee.'[7]

Such magnates would have given little thought to their route; they would simply have arranged the most suitable passage upon the Donaghadee packet-boats. A 1776 letter survives from Sir James Caldwell of Castle Caldwell to the great actor David Garrick advising him how to get to Fermanagh from the Donaghadee packet.[8]

Many wealthy Irish ladies and gentlemen undertook the long packet-boat and coach journey to the fashionable spa at Bath. During his own visits, Daniel Delacherois became so enamoured of baths and bathing (and the money they could bring in!) that he constructed his own hotel and sea-water baths in Donaghadee.[9]

During the turbulent 1790s a number of English and Scottish Fencible Regiments landed in Donaghadee, and both Generals Gerard Lake and George Nugent would surely have climbed up Kelly's Steps to embark upon their tours of duty.[10]

This milepost stands in the Cottown, two Irish miles from Donaghadee. The town's own milepost was lost in the 1990s when the footpath it stood on collapsed into the sea.

Eighteenth century Bath. Charmed by Bath, and not too proud to make money out of hypochondria, Daniel Delacherois built a spa hotel in Donaghadee. (Bath Reference Library)

The port was closed during the 1798 Rebellion. A clue that its re-opening was accompanied by a more determined security policy is given by a unique document. Richard Dill's passport, signed by James Arbuckle and dated 1803, is one of what must have been many such documents. It permitted him to travel to Scotland to study for the Presbyterian ministry.[11]

Over a decade later, the great poet John Keats wrote a long letter to his brother Tom,[12] telling him about his days in Donaghadee, staying in Mr Kelly's neat *Downshire Arms*. He stated that Ireland had less poverty but possibly more jollity than Scotland, illustrating this with a comment about his chambermaid at the inn, who 'is fair, kind and ready to laugh because she is out of the horrible dominion of the Scotch Kirk.'

Travellers' resources varied hugely. Local incomes ranged from the £5000 in annual rents due to landlord David Ker of Portavo, to the shilling a day (or maybe £10-15 a year) earnings of his labourers, and below. Ker often paid half a guinea as a cabin passenger to Portpatrick.

If he took his four-wheeled barouche with him (and how could he do without it?) it would cost Ker another £1 11s 6d, with an additional half guinea each for the horses to pull it. Any travelling servants would have cost him a five-shilling

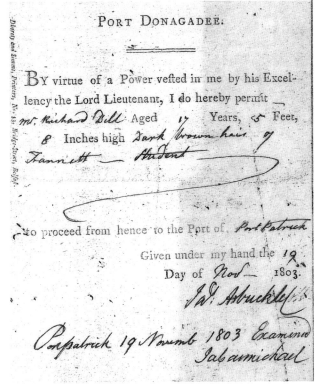

Like many others, Richard Dill was issued with this passport in 1803, when he passed through security conscious, post-Rebellion Donaghadee. (PRONI)

fare each. The harbour men would have charged Ker a half guinea for slinging his carriage onto the packet, and sixpence each for his horses and all his travelling trunks; a grand total of almost £4 for himself, two footmen and the vehicle. On the other hand, a hold passenger would have paid two shillings, and an extra twopence if he needed to be hoisted on board on the sling.

Saving lives
It is a truism that difficult times bring out the best and the worst in people. This is nowhere better evidenced than on a sea coast, where moving water meets solid land, and forms of transport built for one element have to contend with sudden contact with the other.

Between fifty and one hundred shipwrecks have been recorded on the coasts near Donaghadee.[13] There have been many more 'close shaves'. In 1802, for

The 1884 Mew Island lighthouse, which saved countless lives.

instance, the *Hillsborough* on passage from Portpatrick met a sudden heavy squall, 'two planks of the deck under water.' The *Hillsborough* was just managing, but a lady passenger was not. A sudden gust of wind threw her overboard and she disappeared under the ship's keel.

The Captain coolly ran to the lee side of the *Hillsborough* and hung from the rigging with his foot dangling in the sea. The drowning woman had the presence of mind to grab his foot and hold on until members of the crew could haul her back on board.[14]

In November 1807, Captain Hamilton Cranston set out in the *Downshire* for Portpatrick with her usual cargo of mails and passengers. Halfway across she was caught by a 'perfect hurricane' and forced to stand over to the Cumberland coast. She beat her way to shelter in the lee of the Isle of Man. When the storm abated, she was able to proceed to Portpatrick. There she docked with crew, passengers and mails all safe – only eight and a half days late – and on a ship with no catering facilities and only the most rudimentary of privy conveniences! On the following day she returned to Donaghadee in a more typical two hours and ten minutes.[15]

Three years after this adventure, the *Downshire* was obliged to sail from Donaghadee in another heavy north-easterly gale because all her sister ships were cowering in Portpatrick and unable to leave port. When the *Downshire* reached the Scottish terminal she was told not to attempt to dock. She unloaded her mails safely into a small boat, and received three British mails that had been waiting. Then she tried to wear ship in the difficult waters just outside Portpatrick's harbour, but struck a rock to the north.

The obvious solution of limping into Portpatrick harbour was not open to Cranston because this would have tied all four packets to the Scottish coast. He was forced to sail for Ireland. But conditions worsened. Gradually the *Downshire* began to go down. In a remarkable display of courage, several boats came out to try and aid the stricken vessel. But sadly, the ship was lost and one passenger was drowned.

However, the precious mails were saved. The *Belfast News Letter* rejoiced that the letters and parcels were taken into Portpatrick to be dried and sent on to their destinations.[16] Just over six months later it reported that a new *Downshire* was being built at Chester.[17] It is only fitting that the new packet was placed under the command of Captain Cranston.

Another interesting story concerns a sloop that foundered just off Islandmagee in November 1772. The *Lady Loup* from Scotland had foundered on the Gobbins with the loss of eight people. The disaster provoked an outcry when the wreck's three survivors declared that the want of a reliable light on the Copeland Islands had been the cause of their destruction, and demanded that the magistrates and controllers of the lighthouse:

remove forever out of the Copeland Islands the present lightman, his friends, his family and effects, he being a worthless idle villain.[18]

The charge was an extremely grave one, but the truth of it was never established. There certainly *should* have been a light on the Copelands. There had been a brazier on Lighthouse Island since 1715. If its fire was not lit that night then it probably *was* the fault of the keeper, although it should be remembered that it was when ships were most in danger that fires were most difficult to keep lit.

Such disasters persuaded the Irish Lights to replace the coal-fired brazier in 1796. In 1815 they commissioned George Halpin to build a much brighter replacement light only yards from the first. In 1884 they erected the present light on nearby Mew Island. The light is now fully automated, and one of the most powerful in the world.[19]

But what if a light could not prevent a shipwreck? How ready were people to help a ship in dire straits? In 1791 the *Belfast News Letter* carried the following inspiring report:

Sea rescue was a perilous business. Before engines were invented, rowing yawls such as the Lucy, *shown here with William George Nelson and Robert McDowell at the prow, were used to help stricken ships. (Hugh Nelson)*

In the port of Donaghadee, there is a band of resolute seamen, whose sole business is to assist vessels in and out of port, and to go off in yawls to pilot strangers into Belfast. Too much merit cannot be attributed, nor too much praise given, to men who boldly risk their lives in the worst weather, and at all hours of the night, to preserve the lives and properties of their fellow creatures. In February 1780, no less than eleven Donaghadee men were lost in helping the *Amazon* to Belfast.[20]

Some took heroic steps to save human life – others took what they could. Many were guided by a mixture of both motives. After any survivors were safely brought to shore, the wreck itself was often regarded as bounty offered up by the gods of the sea. Stories are told about the pillaging of wrecks from Cornwall to the north of Scotland and further afield. It was no different along the Irish coasts, as this sobering account from 1812 shows us:

Travelling on Thursday 17th December, along the coast [near] Donaghadee I beheld a sight new to me. A brig from Greenock, bound for South America was cast on shore on a point of land [Orlock?]. The shore was crowded with upwards of 500 persons, all of them eagerly engaged in dragging on shore, trunks, boxes, bales, and whatever came to hand. Generous people! I exclaimed.

Scarcely had the words escaped my lips than I was alarmed by the report of Fire-arms; and a ball whistling past at a short distance. People were assembling, many from seven miles distance, in order to plunder and carry off what they could. This they attempted in defiance of a strong guard of soldiers and Customhouse officers.

Covered with the veil of night, the neighbouring farmers, men of substantial property, came with their servants and horses, not to pilfer a web or two but in order to carry off unopened boxes, trunks and bales. Those whose duty it was to protect the property not only connived at these proceedings but actually sold them the goods; and in many instances assisted in loading their carts and cars; besides these they carried off many of the most valuable articles themselves.

Nor is this all, the most disgraceful part remains yet to be told. There were seen engaged in this scene of plunder, sea-faring men, masters and owners of vessels, some of them rich and hitherto respectable. I have given you this statement to publish [that] it might put some of those concerned to shame.[21]

The *Betsey* of Portrush was wrecked on Copeland Island on the day after Boxing Day, 1815. Within hours, her cargo of tallow and her crew had disappeared. A Portrush man made the trip to Donaghadee to discover what he could. He found his friend's underwear hanging in one of the island's houses. A child told him that the bodies of the *Betsey's* crewmen had been buried in the sand, but she did not know just where.

The wreck of the Meridian *and the iron clipper* Ulrica *(shown here) prompted the establishment of an RNLI station in Donaghadee. (North Down Heritage Centre)*

When the *Ulrica* was wrecked on the Copelands in 1897 there were calls for an RNLI lifeboat station to be built in Donaghadee. These efforts intensified four years later when the barque *Meridian* foundered. Seamen like William George Nelson, Captain Robert McDowell and Robert Bunting and local noteables such as Colonel Daniel Louis Delacherois, D.H. Hughes of Coondara, and the rector, the Rev. Henry Coote, leant their weight to the campaign.

The station opened in 1910, with the lifeboat *William and Laura*. Within six years the crew had received an accolade from a surprising quarter. In March 1916, the President of France presented them with a silver medal for saving the crew of a French cargo ship in the Irish Sea.

In 1949, the old lifeboat was succeeded by the *Sir Samuel Kelly*.[22] It would soon see action. On a foul and stormy night the Stranraer-Larne car-ferry went down in heart-rending circumstances. She was, of course, the *Princess Victoria*.

On January 31st 1953, the *Princess Victoria* had set out from Scotland with 127 passengers and forty-nine crew. After hours of relentless buffeting, heavy seas forced open the ship's car doors. When the seawater surged in, many

The Sir Samuel Kelly *in 1953, with crew-members Hugh Nelson (Coxswain), Alex Nelson, Jim Armstrong, Sammy Nelson, John Trimble, Hugh Nelson Junr., Frank Nelson, William Nelson, George Lindsay & Samuel Herron. (Hugh Nelson)*

vehicles broke loose. This tipped the *Princess Victoria* onto its side, and from that point the ship was doomed. At 8.45am Captain James Ferguson contacted the coastguard with a mayday message.

Ships in the area were alerted. RAF aircraft were sent on search missions, and the RNLI lifeboat maroons went up. In the appalling seas the rescuers experienced enormous difficulties both in finding the *Princess Victoria* and in picking up the survivors and the dead.

The *Princess Victoria's* Captain Ferguson had gone down with his ship, but was lauded for his courage. The radio officer, David Broadfoot, was posthumously awarded the George Cross for staying at his post until the ship went down. Of the 176 on board, only forty-three survived. Poignantly, four children under eight were amongst the dead.[23] The living and the dead were carried back to Donaghadee, where the survivors were given medical attention in the Imperial Hotel.[24]

The lifeboat's crew were feted across Ulster, and the lifeboat service later awarded the boat's coxswain, Hugh Nelson, its prestigious Bronze Medal, a fitting companion to the medal that Hugh's brother Sammy had gained for a heroic rescue in Bangor Bay during the war.[25]

4 Eighteenth century Donaghadee

The thriving port

In the eighteenth century, barques and brigs carrying cargo from Scotland usually docked in Belfast, but passengers preferred to travel to and from Donaghadee, because its single-masted sloops and cutters were sleeker and faster. To go from Belfast was a tedious business. To sail from Donaghadee was to travel in style.

Walter Harris has left us with an interesting description of the quay in 1744, when he described it as being:

made of large Stones in Form of a Crescent, without any Cement, and is 128 yards in length, and about 21 or 22 Feet broad, besides a Breast Wall of the same kind of Stones about six feet broad. It affords good shelter to Vessels that lie here from the East and North East Storms, and is capable of receiving twelve or fourteen Bottoms of considerable Bulk. It is the port where the Scottish Packets land.[1]

Harris noted the Presbyterian meeting-house near the shore, and the cruciform Anglican church on its hill, visible, he insists, from Portpatrick. He tells us that a vast number of horses were exported from Donaghadee, 'many of which are stolen'. These were 'generally landed by stealth in the Creeks of Scotland to avoid paying a high Duty there.' He adds that:

the Scotch take from hence sometimes black [or beef] cattle, sheep, wool, wool manufactures, butter... oats and oatmeal, especially in those years when their Harvest in Scotland proves bad.

Half a century later, a French aristocrat, Jacques Louis de Bougrenet, the Chevalier de Latocnaye, visited Donaghadee in the course of two walking

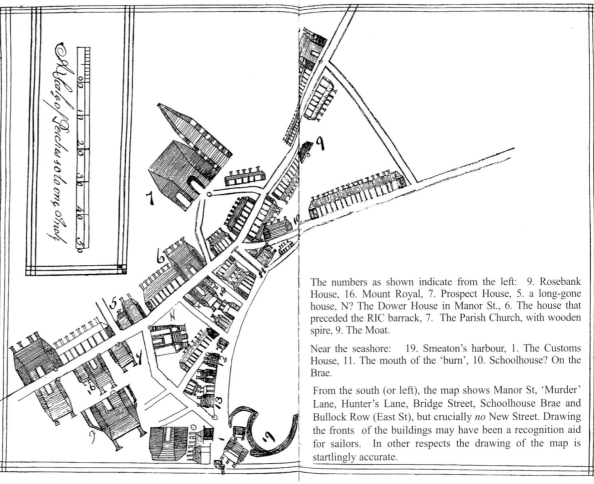

The numbers as shown indicate from the left: 9. Rosebank House, 16. Mount Royal, 7. Prospect House, 5. a long-gone house, N? The Dower House in Manor St., 6. The house that preceded the RIC barrack, 7. The Parish Church, with wooden spire, 9. The Moat.

Near the seashore: 19. Smeaton's harbour, 1. The Customs House, 11. The mouth of the 'burn', 10. Schoolhouse? On the Brae.

From the south (or left), the map shows Manor St, 'Murder' Lane, Hunter's Lane, Bridge Street, Schoolhouse Brae and Bullock Row (East St), but crucially *no* New Street. Drawing the fronts of the buildings may have been a recognition aid for sailors. In other respects the drawing of the map is startlingly accurate.

tours of Ireland. He was particularly struck by the number of young couples fleeing illiberal Ulster to be married in the ceremony-free Scots manner. He was also overwhelmed by the sheer noise and bustle of the port, and echoing Harris, noted that:

The number of cattle taken from here to Scotland is something inconceivable, and the farmers are obliged to submit to the impudent impositions of the owners of the

Dillon's mid(?)-eighteenth century plan of Donaghadee, the earliest known map of the town.

James Boswell, the biographer of Samuel Johnson in a portrait painted four years before his visit. Boswell arrived with amorous intent.

boats that take the cattle. They ask as much as twenty guineas for a crossing, and as they hold the farmer in the hollow of their hands, he is obliged to pay what they ask, and this means that the cost of transport for horned cattle is as much as one guinea per beast... On the day I crossed there were four hundred horned cattle taken over to Scotland, and in the six weeks previous there had been transported nearly thirty thousand.[2]

Boswell in search of a wife

Another notable eighteenth century visitor was the author and biographer James Boswell, who was born in the small town of Auchinleck, not far from Portpatrick, where he was a son of the local laird. Before producing his monumental *Life of Johnson* in 1791, Boswell wrote a most unusual tour of the British Isles called *Boswell in Search of a Wife*. Its style is gossipy and indiscreet, and it includes an amusing account of a visit to Donaghadee.

Boswell arrived in May 1769. He was 'put up at the *Hillsborough Arms* and there drank a dish of tea'. He rode on horseback on a 'fine strand on which a race might be run', and went to nearby Killaghy to call on his aunt, the wife of the Donaghadee Customs Collector, Hugh Boyd.

His object in visiting Ireland, however, was not to visit his aunt, fond as he was of her, but to see a young lady called Mary Ann, with whom he seems to have been in love. He believed that his feelings were reciprocated, 'as her little bosom beats at the thought of seeing me,' and mentions that, if they marry, she will bring him quite a fortune.

He thinks his father will never agree, but declaims that 'if *her* father gives me a round sum, I do not fear *mine.*' He then adds that he is accompanied on his travels by his first cousin, Miss Montgomerie, whom he declares 'perhaps may and perhaps ought to prevent my Hibernian nuptials.' He declares that he is also exceedingly in love with her, but cannot marry her as 'she is two years older than I, [and] has only a thousand pounds.'

One evening, his Aunt Boyd took him and Miss Montgomerie to the town's Manor House for tea *and* supper with the septuagenarian Countess of Mount Alexander, Marie Angélique Delacherois, a Mr Semphill, and both his eligible daughters. However, it was not one of the Semphill girls who took the fickle Boswell's fancy, but the elderly Countess, who at the time of Boswell's visit had been a widow for twelve years. He writes that he amused his 'wild fancy for a moment with thinking how clever it would be for me to carry off the old lady and her great fortune, for which I might well spare a few years.'[3]

But it was not to be. Boswell did not become the new lord of Donaghadee. Marie Angélique died childless two years later, bequeathing her 'fortune' to Daniel Delacherois. Mary Ann married someone else. Margaret Montgomerie was also from a prominent family, and was likely to inherit a title at least. Boswell chose her, and they married shortly after his return from Ireland. They had seven children. Margaret died of tuberculosis in 1789 and Boswell died six years later, at the age of fifty-five.[4]

Who ran Donaghadee?

The 1764 'census' counted 1,948 persons in Donaghadee parish, 1,848 of them Dissenters (or Presbyterians) and the remainder Anglicans.[5] Well under half of this number will have lived in the town. Most of Donaghadee's population then lived in single-storey cottages, roofed with local Ballygrainey slate, and held with long vegetable gardens, and worked in one of the many trades needed in a busy seaport and fishing town.

As the nineteenth century approached, Daniel Delacherois and his successors, as local magistrates and Lords of the Manor, would have overseen much of the daily governance of the town – the keeping of the law, the controlling of livestock, even the orderly removal of seaweed from the foreshore for manure.

Everyday things such as roads, burials and the like were the responsibility of the civil parish. The Anglican and Presbyterian churches also exerted a considerable informal influence on local life and mores. They tried to ensure that everyone was baptised, married, educated, and generally well-behaved.

There were other men who exerted influence on the town and townspeople. We have already met some of them. One was David Ker of Portavo, the district's wealthiest landowner.[6] Another was Robert Stewart, First Earl of Londonderry, the most powerful man in the Ards.[7] Both ensured that their voices were heard on matters affecting them or their property. Arthur Hill, Earl of Hillsborough, later Marquis of Downshire, was another locally influential grandee. Downshire was the largest landowner in County Down, and one of the most influential men in Ireland.[8] He chaired the board of the Donaghadee Packet Company and was consulted on every matter pertaining to it.

These men, however, were primarily interested in the port, rather than the town, and we need to draw a clear distinction between the two. The port was owned by the Packet company. The town was owned and largely

The most powerful man in the Ards'. Robert Stewart, First Marquis of Londonderry, minus wig, in later life. (Ker family)

Donaghadee owed its reputation for fast, reliable travel to Scotland to vessels like this cutter. Cutters were 'faster than anything bigger', in spite of wearing their suit of sail on a single mast.

administered by the Delacherois family. In some ways the town was the junior partner. James Arbuckle, whom we shall meet shortly, believed the busy port to be attached to a mere 'hamlet'.[9]

He had a point. The port's influence was pervasive, and the servicing of the port and its shipping was arguably the main business of the town. The port itself was run by a small band of officials. The packet service and Royal Mail franchise were important enough for the port to boast the positions of Surveyor and Customs Collector. These men did not just maintain the harbour and collect the revenue due for using it. They ruled the port, and ruled it with an iron hand. Nothing happened within it that they and Downshire did not know about.

These officials were not appointed after an open selection process. This was an era of patronage. Anyone seeking a post would send a fawning letter enclosing references to the patron in whose gift the position lay. If he were considered suitable he would receive the position, possibly for life. Applicants included superannuated career soldiers, naval officers, and well-educated but only comfortably-off young men.

In 1786, an ambitious young gentleman called William Hull wrote to Downshire's son, Lord Hillsborough, thoughtfully pointing out that Mr Lyle, the Port Surveyor, appeared not to be too long for this world.[10] He suggested that a successor would soon be needed, and commended himself for the post. Within weeks he had his appointment. A few years later, he secured the position of Secretary of the Packet Company for his son, Edward.

Edward Hull and his wife Elizabeth had four sons between 1801-04. They were careful to baptise them John Dawson, William Trevor, Arthur Hill and Edward Leslie after the powerful men whose patronage these sons might one day seek to call on. By 1803 Hull was using the honorific, 'Esq.' after his name, and 'Surveyor' as his occupation.[11]

Edward Hull continued in both of his posts for many years. By 1824 he had become a magistrate, and Acting-Collector at the new Customs House, which stood beside his fine dwelling-house in Meetinghouse Street.[12] In later years, ill health obliged Hull to retire to the Isle of Wight. He died a lonely old man in 1845, never to know that four years later, the government contract for carrying the mails on his beloved packet boats would be withdrawn.

The most colourful of the port's officials was James Arbuckle, who applied for the position of Customs Collector in 1786.[13] Arbuckle was not then a young man. In 1759 he had married, then spent some fifteen years looking after his family's Maryvale estate near Newry, hoping that some position would turn up. His close friend, Dr. William Drennan, tells us that Arbuckle was 'a man of taste and a very pleasing gentleman', and that he would 'be satisfied in getting [a post] worth £200 per annum.'[14]

Arbuckle must have convinced Lord Hillsborough that he was right for the position because it was not long before he filled it. He was an excellent choice. Ably assisted by his loyal deputy, Pro-Collector William Getty,[15] Arbuckle served for over thirty-five years, dying in office in 1823, at the great age of eighty-nine.

Five years after his appointment, Arbuckle lost his wife Mary.[16] For years he had been on good terms with the Earl of Roden, often visiting his magnificent Tollymore Park home.[17] After the death of his wife, Arbuckle seems to have paid a little more serious attention to Roden's six daughters. By the mid 1790s he had become married to one of them – the Honourable Lady Sophia Jocelyn.

If Arbuckle had ever held any doubt about his social status, this marriage ended it. With his father-in-law's help, the Arbuckles were soon living in some style at Ballywilliam House, just off the road to Groomsport, where they remained until James's death.

Arbuckle wrote often to Downshire. His letters display both his intense loyalty to the Crown and his hugely entertaining bad temper.[18] During the difficult 1790s he could scarcely contain his contempt for what he regarded as incendiary Presbyterian clerics such as James Porter of Greyabbey, and William Steel Dickson of Portaferry. He was equally hard on his fellow loyalists, lashing even his social superiors when they were too timid to act in times of difficulty, with a gleeful disregard for the possible consequences. He also disapproved of Donaghadee's most successful businessman and Seneschal, James Lemon, a man Arbuckle suspected of Presbyterian republicanism:

This foolish fellow, and there cannot well be a more foolish than James Lemon, does a deal of mischief by babbling and prating in his shop to the lower class.[19]

In a letter to Downshire, he even had the temerity to reveal his true thoughts about Robert Stewart's attempts to quell the spirit of rebellion in the Ards, possibly feeling safe in the knowledge that the two noblemen had no love for each other:

Arbuckle's 'arch enemy', the liberal, reform-minded James Lemon, the Seneschal of Donaghadee. (Private collection)

I was astounded at the precipitancy and weakness of the measures attempted to be enforced by my neighbouring Earl Londonderry. The family is now I think the most unpopular in the country.[20]

As in de Latocnaye's France a few years earlier, the gulf between rich and poor in Ireland was dangerously large and the population was increasing rapidly. In these circumstances, Ireland's great landlords cannot have been entirely surprised when they began to hear stories of a growing discontent. In areas like the Ards, where the majority of the population were Dissenters, what was perceived as an unfair exercise of power by the established church and gentry stoked rising tensions, tensions that were soon to explode.

5 The great new harbour

The 1798 Rebellion

In April 1797, after being tipped off by an informer, government troops raided clandestine meetings of the United Irishmen in a Belfast tavern. The rebels and their secret papers were captured. Amongst these were the so-called 'Donaghadee Resolutions'.

These resolutions asserted that power lay with the people, and that if rulers degenerated into tyrants, the people were entitled to reclaim their rights, by force of arms if necessary.[1]

No one knows why they were called the 'Donaghadee Resolutions', but they certainly served as an alarm-call for the government. The threat to authority would come not from the long-dreaded French invasion, but from the enemy within.

A determined attempt to recruit a yeomanry corps and break up the united Irish movement followed. Arbuckle made himself deeply unpopular as he became Donaghadee's loudest voice against the growing support for the United Irishmen.[2] But the measures taken by Arbuckle and others only postponed the Rebellion. In June 1798, the fomenting boil of discontent burst. Rebel detachments fought the crown forces at Saintfield, Portaferry, Newtownards and Ballynahinch.

As the neighbouring gentry (including Arbuckle!) fled to Scotland, the local United Irishmen seized the strategic port of Donaghadee, holding the town and its barrack for almost a week. When the decisive charge at the Battle of Ballynahinch scattered the Ardsmen to the hilly refuge of Slieve Croob, the flames of rebellion in the north were quelled. Show trials and executions in

The Battle of Ballynahinch. This defeat of the United Irishmen of County Down, although a 'near-run thing', crushed the spirit of rebellion in the north of Ireland. (Office of Public Works, Dublin)

many County Down towns then snuffed out any remaining sparks.[3]

The uprising stilled the port. Trade in and out of Donaghadee virtually ceased for about a year after the Rebellion, and it would take two more years for commerce to recover, with trade down to about a quarter of what it was before.[4]

The port's fate in the balance

But it was not only the social and commercial fabric that was crumbling. In March 1796, Edward Hull informed Lord Downshire that the bad winter weather had grievously damaged the quay:

If assistance [from government] is not soon obtained it is the general opinion that it will go to ruin. In its present state it can hardly stand two such winters as the last...[5]

Little if anything was done. But Hull did not let the matter rest. Eight months before the Rebellion he complained that:

the situation of our Quay grows every day worse and worse. Mr Smith [Donaghadee's Postmaster and the Packet Company's Treasurer] cannot be prevailed on to lay out anything on it.[6]

For a time, the cataclysmic events of 1798, and the Act of Union of 1800, overshadowed the matter of the harbour. Ten anxious years would pass before its difficulties were properly addressed.

As peace gradually returned to Ireland, it became clear that government money would have to be spent on modern harbours at either end of the Short Sea Passage. The House of Lords appointed a select committee to determine the two optimum locations for its terminals. The committee's first task was to discover just how much commerce there actually was on the route.

Arbuckle was asked to provide up-to-date information on imports and exports across the North Channel. The figures he produced are most illuminating. They show that for the years 1801-07 an average of 478 cargo-carrying ships brought 25,358 tons of goods out of Donaghadee each year, while 396 ships brought in cargoes of 20,211 tons.[7] Most of these cargo vessels were of 46-53 tons burden – a range likely to have been dictated by the small size of the harbour.

Donaghadee's major export was oxen. These animals arrived from all over Ulster, and even from Leinster and Connaught, to be driven down Bullock Row (now East Street) to the Bullock Slip on the foreshore. At low tide the beasts were goaded up the ramps of sturdily-built wooden vessels and shipped to Scotland. In written histories of the time these animals are often invisible, but these beasts must have been an awesome sight as they were driven in their hundreds along the narrow dirt roads.

When the cattle reached Portpatrick they resumed their walking tour to the markets of Great Britain, rejoicing in their new nationality as 'Scotch cattle'. For two centuries, these beasts represented over half of all exports out of Donaghadee, making the port Ulster's equivalent of an American prairie railhead a century later.

The town's other conspicuous export was horses. From travellers' descriptions, it is easy to imagine great equine herds being shipped to England, to serve as mounts for cavalry regiments. However, the third biggest transport category was 'carriages &c.' suggesting that, although many of the horses were headed for market, a number of them pulled the numerous carriages that were shipped to and fro across the Irish Sea.

What of the incoming vessels? A small number imported coal from the Ayrshire and Cumbrian fields. A few were fishing vessels loaded with herrings from off the Isle of Man. Nine out of ten of the remaining boats came from Portpatrick.

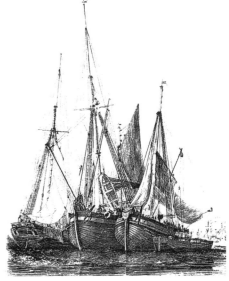

Sturdy smacks like these were invaluable for cargo-carrying. They keeled over in dry harbours so that livestock could be walked on and off.

Portpatrick, Donaghadee's 'sister' port. The presence of the cutters suggests that this view predates 1825. (Donaghadee & Portpatrick)

It is an indication of the importance of the cattle exports that two thirds of the ships carrying these beasts to Scotland could find no worthwhile cargoes to carry back, and were forced to return in no-profit ballast.

The figures show Donaghadee to have been a small but relatively busy port, even discounting the Packet Boat business. They also make clear that government assistance would be essential if the port was to develop further.

Which brings us back to the 1808 Inquiry. This revealed problems with the Short Sea Passage as currently constituted, problems that begged fundamental questions. Either the route was fine, but the ports of Donaghadee and Portpatrick needed improvement, or the route was bad, and new harbours *and* a new route were needed. Donaghadee's privileged status was thrown into jeopardy.

The government commissioned the most famous engineer of the day, Thomas Telford, to determine the best possible route. He was to explore every possible harbour site on each side of the route and report back. Telford received a flurry of self-interested submissions from local landowners. In addition to the two most obvious port candidates of Portpatrick and Donaghadee, cases were made for the almost unknown Ardwell Bay and Port Nessock on the Scottish side, and Bangor and Portavo on the Irish side.

Enemies of the existing route advised abandoning Portpatrick because of its vulnerability to the prevailing winds, and David Ker presented ambitious plans aimed at turning the Portavo foreshore into the busiest port in the north of Ireland.

Those who favoured Bangor industriously chased up 240 ship's captains, who lodged a petition, endorsed by Telford himself, stating that Bangor-Port Nessock was a quicker and better route, although twice as long.

Telford's summation was less than judicious. He presented detailed criticisms of every aspect of the ports of Donaghadee and Portpatrick, and of the sea route between them, and then extolled the dubious virtues of Bangor and Port Nessock.

At the inquiry, Edward Hull answered Telford's charges in a masterly fashion. He dealt with each point in turn, e.g. the relative distances, the contrary prevailing winds, the rock-bound approaches to Bangor versus uninterrupted deep water on the existing route, etc. It was a virtuoso performance. Telford's arguments were demolished. The committee adjourned to consider its findings.

Thomas Telford's intended harbour, 1808. Telford's plan cut across the local geography, Rennie's flowed with it, making excellent use of the rocky outcrops of 'Little Scotland' shown here. For all the attractions of Rennie's scheme, many sailors believe that Telford's would have made the better harbour. (British and Foreign Harbours)

The shape of the future. In ten short years steamers or 'smokeboats' ceased to be curiosities and became fast and reliable passenger ferries.

Their conclusion was not foregone. Bangor and Carrickfergus each had their advocates, and many within Ireland's administration remained angry with the Donaghadee authorities for having lost control of the port during the insurrection. After months of deliberation, the committee concluded:

that the passage between the two Kingdoms would be greatly facilitated and accelerated by the improvement of the harbours of Port Patrick and Donaghadee.[8]

Donaghadee would get a new lease of life.

The new harbour

On an otherwise unremarkable day in 1815, just about everyone in Donaghadee hurried down to the quayside upon hearing that a wonder was at hand. There they saw the awesome sight of the 105 ton *S.S. Caledonia* cruising past the Copelands on her way from the Clyde to London. It was the first time any of them had seen a steamship.[9] What no-one realised at the time was the huge impact that 'smokeboats' like the *Caledonia* would have on Donaghadee.

In the same year, a second inquiry endorsed the 1809 decision. Thomas Telford's arch-rival, John Rennie, was appointed architect of the new harbours at Portpatrick and Donaghadee.[10]

Rennie, a Scottish engineer from Phantassie, near East Linton, was well known for his work on bridges, harbours, and the Royal Canal from Dublin to the River Shannon. The Marquis of Downshire (who else!) was appointed Chairman of the Harbour Commissioners, and in February 1821 work commenced at Donaghadee. On Wednesday July 31st 1821, the Marquis, accompanied by his wife and son, performed the symbolic act of laying the foundation stone. When Downshire arrived on Tuesday afternoon, the harbour workmen:

having learnt that his Lordship was expected, went a mile out of town, where they stopped his carriage, and, took off the horses and drew his Lordship and his family, amidst loud acclamations to the house of Mr Hull, where, after giving three hearty cheers, they returned to their work in the greatest order.[11]

Hull was the man who had first recognised the need for a newer and better harbour, and done the greatest part of the work needed to bring it about. His position entitled him to the first hosting at his Meetinghouse Street home. Mrs Hull and her staff made a special dinner for the many guests assembled. The following morning, Rennie's workmen gathered outside Hull's house 'dressed

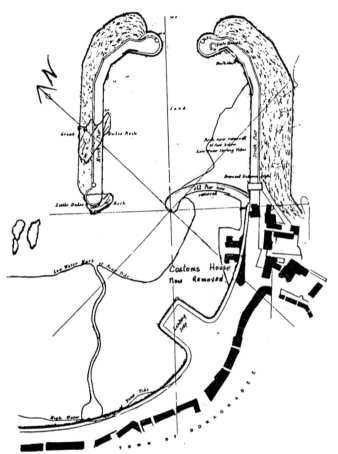

Plan of Rennie's harbour – almost the last to be designed for sailing vessels anywhere in the United Kingdom. His drawing also shows the old, banana-shaped quay and Arbuckle's Customs House.

in their best attire, each of them with new white pantaloons.' A carefully choreographed procession then marched off towards the Parade.

Hundreds had swarmed into the great amphitheatre inside which the ceremony was to be held. All the great and the good of the day were present. Downshire, Hull, David Logan, the resident superintending engineer, the Harbour Commissioners, and most of the ladies and gentlemen from miles around, all walking in procession in a strictly designated order.

Downshire told the crowd the history of the harbour, and emphasised the great wealth that the new harbour would bring to all parts of the United

Elevation

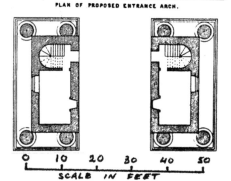

PLAN OF PROPOSED ENTRANCE ARCH.

SCALE IN FEET

Rennie wanted to crown Donaghadee's harbour with a magnificent, four-storied arch not unlike the Arc de Triomphe *in Paris. Alas, this towering structure was never built.*

Kingdom. Prayers were said for the success of the project. Then the Marquis laid the foundation stone with an inscribed silver trowel.

This stone has never been lifted. Beneath it, to this day, lie a silver plate, assorted testimonials, and a glass bottle containing coins bearing the likeness of George IV. When the ceremony ended, the ladies and gentlemen repaired to the ballroom in the Market House. Here, Mrs Delacherois served the company 'an elegant cold collation' and later took a favoured few back to the Manor House to relax before the grand dinner and ball she had arranged for that evening. The new harbour had got off to a most auspicious start.

Two months after work started, the great John Rennie died. The Commissioners lost no time in appointing his twenty-seven year old son, John Rennie Junior as Principal Engineer in his place, or as they put it, 'in the room of his late father', with David Logan to continue as Resident Engineer at Donaghadee.[12]

Just like his father, Rennie sought limestone from Moelfre in Anglesey for the public front of the harbour, and iron-hard greywacke-sandstone of Donaghadee for the remainder of the works. When Sir Humphrey Davy, President of the Royal Society, had been shown the Quarry Hole on his way through Donaghadee, he had told Rennie that its Ordovician graywacke was 'fully equal to any stone hitherto used at any public work.' All the limestone blocks were finished locally, and the chippings burned for lime mortar.[13] This work was done on ground just above Salt Pan Bay, which became known as 'the Hewin' Fields.'

To protect the ongoing works from the sea, Rennie sequestered them within a roughly square, stone, clay and rubble dam, which enclosed 'nearly an acre' of what had been open sea. A staggering 600,000 cubic feet of greywacke bedrock was removed by men using cranes, carts and a horse-drawn railway. The sea-water was then pumped out, and the Packet Company's agent, James Lemon, reported that there was not one leak in the entire coffer dam.[14] As the packets passed the new dyke, the crewmen on deck were able to gaze down upon the harbour workers waving to them from the floor of the new works an amazing thirty-six feet below.

On May 21st 1825, it was time for the sea to resume its rightful place. The simple ceremony comprised a salute of cannon fire and a band playing *Rule Britannia* and other martial airs.[15] There was no sign of the sea-bed banquet so popular in fireside tales. The great harbour basin was simply too wet and too dangerous for such frivolities.

Rennie also calls another cherished piece of Donaghadee folklore into question. This is the idea that the tiny stone 'castle' on top of Donaghadee's Moat, built in 1819, was used as a gunpowder magazine for the harbour. Rennie's 1822 report is unequivocal on the subject, stating that no powder magazine was necessary as powder came regularly from Belfast in small quantities, a practice he thought altogether safer.[16] The castle was sometimes marked as a Magazine on later maps, so may have become such later, or indeed it may simply have been an exuberant, romantic folly.

As the work neared completion, the packets began to berth in the new harbour, until eventually Smeaton's old harbour was cleared of all its dock furniture and simply blasted away.

Rennie described Donaghadee harbour as having been begun in 1821 and completed in 1836.[17] This was a reference to the authorities' initial refusal to sanction a lighthouse on Donaghadee's south pier. But the Commissioners of Irish Lights relented,[18] and on the night of January 11th 1836 a fixed light shone at the end of the south pier for the first time. Donaghadee had acquired its famous limestone lighthouse! Initially, its stone stood unvarnished. But it has been regularly painted white for about a century (once, famously, by Brendan Behan in the 1950s). In 1934, this lighthouse was the first in Ireland to be electrified.

For his work on the harbour, and other achievements, Rennie was awarded a knighthood – something that his homespun father had steadfastly declined. But he must have left Donaghadee feeling some frustration. For the harbour's architectural *piece de resistance*, a magnificent triumphal arch, was never built, because of a shortage of money.[19]

6 The communications revolution

Brand new smokeboats

A year after the completion of the harbour, an exciting advertisement appeared in the *Belfast News Letter*. It let the whole world know that the wind was no longer blowing favourably on the Short Sea Crossing:

The end of an era. Extract from the Belfast News Letter *of July 25th 1825.*

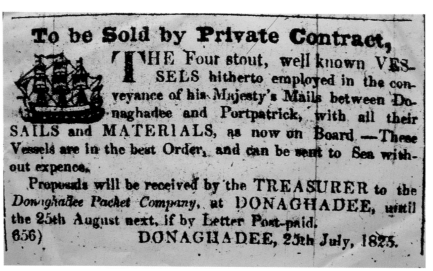

To be Sold by Private Contract,

THE Four stout, well known VES-SELS hitherto employed in the conveyance of his Majesty's Mails between Donaghadee and Portpatrick, with all their SAILS and MATERIALS, as now on Board.—These Vessels are in the best Order, and can be sent to Sea without expence.

Proposals will be received by the TREASURER to the *Donaghadee Packet Company*, at DONAGHADEE, until the 25th August next, if by Letter Post-paid.

856)   DONAGHADEE, 25th July, 1825.

The redundant vessels were cutters – the fastest and most efficient single-masted sailers one could find, and they had been decommissioned by the Packet Company a few weeks earlier. In 1821, Nicholas Batt, the President of

Belfast Chamber of Commerce, had advocated the use of steamboats on the route to Portpatrick.[1] The initiative won the Packet Company's approval. It decided to put its faith in steam.

This had not been what Rennie had intended. He had designed Donaghadee for sailing ships, as the scarlet rings still visible on the pier walls and near Kelly's Steps confirm. And he insisted upon keeping the rings, even though steamships had no need to be warped out of harbour using rings and winches like a sailing ship did. In time, however, many of the rings were unceremoniously removed.

In 1825, the new-fangled, steam-powered *Dasher* and *Arrow* were crossing from Portpatrick to Donaghadee in two and a half hours, with an impressive disregard for the wind.[2] Cutters continued to ply the route, and under some conditions, the wind could get under the skirts of the cutters and fling them along much quicker than the steady six or seven knots of the steamers.

Warping rings are an unmistakable sign of a harbour designed for sailing ships. These ships left the harbour by winching themselves diagonally to and fro until they cleared all obstacles and could hoist sail.

It is no wonder that in such a breeze the seamen on a sloop or cutter under jubilant sail on a fine broad reach would salute the crew of the new 'smokeboats' with such jolly sailors' gestures as are customary on these occasions. On the return journey into the breeze we may imagine the gestures being enthusiastically returned.

But the technological revolution was underway. Donaghadee's age of sail died that very summer. Over the next twenty years the sluggish *Dasher* and *Arrow* were replaced by the more powerful *Spitfire* and the *Fury* (later named *Pike* and *Asp*).[3] By now the gestures, if there were any, all went the one way.

A harvest of silver
For several years, Moelfre limestone was carried in sturdy cargo boats from Holyhead to Donaghadee. Friendships were struck up between local crewmen and people from Anglesey, and these friendships would have interesting repercussions.

In 1828, one of the packet boats was taken to Holyhead for a refit. While they were there, some of the crew members who had worked on the limestone boats met up with their Welsh friends. There, in Holyhead's dockside taverns, they talked too freely about a secret they had kept to themselves for a quarter of a century.

The following summer some Donaghadee fishermen spotted a Welsh salvage ship named the *Clown* moored a few yards off Mew Island.[4] The ship carried what looked like an enormous bronze bell on her deck. What could it be? As they saw it being hoisted over the *Clown's* side it dawned on them. This was a diving bell. The *Clown's* crew were diving for treasure. Within days, word of its activities became public, and what had been a precious local secret was the talk of Ulster.

Over the next few weeks, the Welshmen recovered ten or fifteen bags of silver dollars from the seabed. The silver was from the *Enterprize*, which a quarter of a century earlier had struck the rocks of Mew Island, while homeward bound for Liverpool.[5]

Only seven out of its crew of eighteen had been saved. The few eye-witnesses to the disaster had watched in amazement as, instead of struggling ashore, some of the stricken ship's crew had come on deck carrying axes, which they used to smash open a large oak barrel that was nailed to the deck.

They were after money. In those days, trading profits were carried home as bullion or coinage in just such a barrel. Greed had made the men lose all reason, even in their extreme peril. A few seconds later, their pockets weighted with silver, these men had jumped into the foaming waves – and gone straight to the seabed and their deaths.

The silver dollars, elephant tusks from Africa, loaves of sugar from Cuba and the stern board proclaiming *Enterprize's* home port left no doubt in anyone's mind. This was a slave trader, a Guineaman homeward bound after completing its lucrative voyage round the 'Slave Triangle'.

As the storm abated, the ship's ribs sank further and further into the sea. Before anyone could make more than a token attempt at salvage, the *Enterprize* was well out of sight below the waves, even at low water. The prize was now too deep to be salvaged. It might as readily have been two hundred feet down. All that locals could do was keep their secret until the sea gave up the silver, or technology came to their aid.

And technology did. By the end of the eighteenth century engineers such as John Smeaton had resuscitated Aristotle's idea of a diving bell, equipped with a force pump for driving down fresh air. In the 1820s Isambard Kingdom Brunel, needing to work underwater to repair his inundated Thames Tunnel turned, by an uncanny coincidence, to John Rennie Junior, who came up with an improved shield and pumping engine.[6]

Downshire's Commissioners described the use of such bells in the excavations at Donaghadee as early as 1823.[7] The Holyhead men had clearly obtained a similar bell, and the stories they had heard had encouraged them to try it off the Copelands. By October 1829 the *Clown* had harvested a truly amazing £50,000 in silver dollars from the seabed off Mew Island.[8] The Donaghadee men were unhappy that all this silver had been salvaged from what they had now come to think of as *their* wreck. It did not take them long to 'persuade' the Welshmen to leave the area.

The Donaghadee men then built their own diving bell. Unlike the bronze bell of the Welshmen, the Donaghadee bell was made of wood. This homemade device was of more practical use than it might first appear. Once their wooden bell had its heavy iron plates and airline attached it was ready for underwater trials. However, when the bell was lowered into the sea it suddenly broke free from its ropes. Those aboard were instantly thrown into the water. All the men were rescued, except for a James Bailie who was never seen again. But the tests continued, and in time the bell was towed to Mew Island. After some discussion, a brave carpenter called John Cornell agreed to try his luck in the bell.[9]

The Welshmen used a diving bell to search for silver dollars. (Elizabeth Taggart)

In the 1830s, diving suits were used to take thousands more dollars from the wreck.

His first dive was fruitless, but he had more luck on his second, when:

observing a cavity in a rock, [Cornell] attempted to put his hand into it, but was prevented by the Ostracion (or box-fish) guarding the portals of its silvery mansion. He slew the monster and took from the cave no less than 180 dollars.

Cornell and his mates never revealed how many dollars they gathered from the *Enterprize*, but the following summer three vessels from Donaghadee, the *Kitty*, the *John*, and the *Industry*, and an unknown ship from Portpatrick were working off Mew Island with diving bells. It isn't known if they found any dollars.

Four years later, a revolutionary new 'Patent Diving Apparatus' was being used to dive for the dollars.[10] A man called Deane had made a 'heavy-footer' diving suit, whereby, through the judicious use of lead weights, a diver could walk on the seabed. The suits must have been a huge improvement, because these late gleaners were able to take another 24,000 dollars from the deep.

The only memento the fortune hunters left in Donaghadee was a limpet-encrusted bottle containing a clear amber liquid. This was put on display in the window of the Lord Nelson Hotel. No modern diver has ever admitted seeing a Mew Island dollar, but even today people still think wistfully of the *Dollarman*, as the *Enterprize* is locally known.[11]

The end of the packet service

Decisive though their findings seemed, the 1808 and 1815 inquiries had not finally settled the matter of the best North Channel route. Now that reliable steamers had demonstrated that the channel could be crossed at any state of wind and tide, places as far apart as Greenock, Ardrossan and Cairnryan on the Scottish side, and Belfast and Larne on the Irish side were being advocated as better suited to a steam mail service. Indeed, in the year that the first steam packets were introduced, a faint note sounding something like a distant death knell was heard:

should the worst happen... packets have only to be sent round to Loch Ryan to ensure the regular conveyance of the mail.[12]

In June 1847, the Admiralty became responsible for maintaining the harbour at Portpatrick. Auckland, the First Sea Lord, seemed content with the status quo. But within two years he had died, and his successor Lord Clanricarde changed the Admiralty's stance. In June 1849, the *Greenock Advertiser* announced that:

government has finally resolved... to supersede the Portpatrick and Donaghadee station. The contract with Messrs. Burns has been signed, and the business begins between this port and Belfast on 16th July.[13]

And so, just like that, the mail service was abruptly transferred to the Belfast-Glasgow route. By December 1849, the Donaghadee Packet Service had gone forever. At the time, however, the decision looked anything but irrevocable, and the next fifteen years saw the same relentless in-fighting about the routes as the previous fifteen. Petitions were sent to the Lords of the Treasury.[14] Donaghadee merchants even rowed from Donaghadee to Portpatrick, then took coaches to Parliament, to demonstrate the ease of passage praised in James I's Charter of 1616.[15]

The arguments continued to and fro with as much energy but with less dignity than the packet boats. For a time, Dublin-Holyhead became the sole mail route across the Irish Sea. Donaghadee pushed for reinstatement or huge compensation, and Larne-Stranraer only became established as late as 1868.[16] From 1851 onwards, railway connections were proposed in an effort to bolster the competing claims. Within the decade lines were laid from Carlisle and Glasgow to Portpatrick, and from Belfast to Donaghadee.

Donaghadee Harbour

After 1849, large steamers were rare visitors. The port's glory days were over. (Robert Neill Collection)

The race for rail

Within two years of losing its status as a packet station, Donaghadee's long time rival, the town of Bangor, overtook it in size for the very first time. Disappointed, even shattered, at the loss of the packet service, the burgers of Donaghadee then watched Bangor make use of the 1854 Towns' Improvement (Ireland) Act to remove its two huge cotton mills. Dirty, smoky Bangor was cleaning itself up in a bid to become Ulster's premier watering-hole. If it was not going to fall even further behind, Donaghadee needed to act.

Population of Bangor and Donaghadee 1841-81

Year	Bangor	Donaghadee
1841	2116	3151
1851	2850	2818
1861	2531	2671
1871	2560	2226
1881	3006	1861

Aware of the enormous prosperity that railways could bring, Donaghadee's entrepreneurs resolved to extend the Belfast-Newtownards railway line to their port, and make a new line from Portpatrick to Carlisle. They would then put state-of-the-art steamers on the waters between the two historic ports, and revive the old sea route's glory days.[17] But Bangor was also gripped by railway mania. The race for rail was on.

Donaghadee won it. By the spring of 1861, a new track, complete with stations and bridges, had almost been completed from Newtownards, through the Six Road Ends, Cannyreagh and the Millisle Road Halt to Donaghadee harbour.[18]

The line had been built for the Belfast & County Down Railway Company (B&CDR) by Edwards of Dublin for the contract price of £50,000. However, the B&CDR had been slow to pay Edwards. This had meant that the contractors could not pay the wages due to their men.

In April 1861, as the Confederate army captured Fort Sumter in Charleston, preparations for the opening ceremony got underway in Donaghadee. On June 1st, the great day arrived. The *Belfast News Letter* waxed lyrical about the quality of the line and track, and the facilities at Donaghadee:

The new station, or terminus, at Donaghadee is neatly constructed, and in order to gain access to it from the street, a house fronting the street was purchased, through which a somewhat handsome entrance has been formed, and portions of the building have been admirably fitted up as waiting-rooms, ticket-office, refreshment-rooms, &c., and the adjoining premises have been taken for an hotel, which is about being opened therein.[19]

Cab, sir? People gather outside the railway station in 1910. (Robert Neill Collection)

Donaghadee station. The tall funnel on locomotive 'No. 1' suggests that this photograph may date from the 1860s, making it the oldest outdoor photograph known from the town. (Day family)

But the newspaper missed the real story. A few mornings before the grand opening, a trial run from Belfast had been organised. This train had been compelled to stop at Newtownards because a large stone and a derailed waggon had been placed across later sections of the track. With the support of their employers, the 'navvies' had also removed one of the rails. They had chosen the perfect time to press for the £6,000 they were owed.

Rattled, the B&CDR promised prompt payment. A few hours later, the first train from Belfast was able to pull into Donaghadee station. However, with the trains now running smoothly, the B&CDR reneged on its promise. None of this reached the ears or eyes of the public.[20] Months afterwards, the Edwards brothers were paid what was due. They must have seen this as a satisfactory outcome, because Edwards went on to build the Holywood-Bangor line, which opened in 1865.

Before the railway opened, the journey to Belfast had taken an arduous five or six hours. After June 1861, it became a rather more comfortable forty minutes.

Under the seabed to Scotland
In 1900, half a century after the sailing of Donaghadee's last packet boat, a bold new plan appeared in the pages of the *Irish Builder*, one that reasserted

Donaghadee's historic custodianship of the North Channel Crossing.[21] A civil engineer named Lynden Livingston Macassey[22] suggested boring a tunnel under the seabed between Scotland and Ulster, within which steam trains could travel.

Macassey's proposal was not entirely revolutionary. A tunnel under the English Channel had been proposed during the Napoleonic Wars, and during the nineteenth century tunnels had been made under the Thames, Severn, and Mersey rivers. There had even been tunnels driven under the Alps at places such as St. Gotthard. But all these tunnels were relatively short. It was over twenty miles from the Ards to Galloway, and the sea was nearly three hundred metres deep.[23] In order to create the slopes necessary to allow trains to go under the seabed and up again on the other side, Macassey's tunnel would need to be forty miles long.[24]

Could this feat be accomplished? Many thought so. Engineers were also considering tunnels from Whitehead to Portpatrick, and Islandmagee to Wierston. Macassey's father, who had famously engineered the Silent Valley reservoir in 1891, had proposed a tunnel between Cushendall and Kintyre. Trial borings were being made with a view to cutting a tunnel between Calais and Dover. A drawing of a putative Donaghadee-Portpatrick tunnel had accompanied a prospectus issued by Daniel Delacherois and a Mr Ormsby in 1886.[25]

Although the geology of the seabed between Ulster and Scotland was then a largely unknown quantity, Macassey deemed the technical problems (maintaining the air pressure, waterproofing the tunnel walls, etc.) surmountable. The only problem, he argued breezily, was finance. He estimated that the tunnel would cost from six to sixteen million pounds. Though it would be to 'the general benefit of trade', he concluded that the enormous price tag might just prohibit its construction. Work has yet to begin.

Macassey, who had as much of the dreamer about him as the engineer, believed that a steam train such as this could travel comfortably in a narrow tunnel to Scotland.

7 A town whose star has fallen?

The Montgomerys

Because of the success of his colony in north Down, Hugh Montgomery was given the title of First Viscount of the Ards. He did not take long to refurbish the castle at the old priory in Newtownards, and later build a grand house near Comber. Here his son, also Hugh, succeeded to the viscountcy in 1636. He named the Comber house Mount Alexander after his wife Jean, the eldest daughter of Sir William Alexander, First Earl of Stirling and Viscount of Canada.[1]

The Third Viscount, yet another Hugh, was elevated to the title of First Earl of Mount Alexander. He was a unique man. In a hunting accident in his youth he had been thrown onto a jagged tree stump, which had opened the wall of his chest. The wound had healed, but the physicians of the day were unable to close the gaping opening. For the remainder of Montgomery's life, the movement of the organs inside his chest could be viewed inside their natural cavity. For obvious reasons, the First Earl always wore a large metal chest-plate under his shirt as protection.

Everyone who heard about this curiosity wanted to look into Montgomery's chest to view the marvels within. In time, word of his medical condition reached the ears of the greatest physician of the day, William Harvey. He astounded Montgomery by telling him that the beating muscle inside his open chest was his heart.

Harvey took the earl to meet Charles I, who followed the practice of hundreds before him by plunging his hand between the separated ribs and deep into the offered cavity. There he was able to hold the living, beating heart in his hand. Montgomery returned to Mount Alexander during Cromwell's Commonwealth, and remained healthy enough to declare Charles II king at Newtownards Market Cross in 1660, but his precarious medical condition meant that he did not live to see his fortieth birthday.

The Second Earl, another Hugh Montgomery, was the man who met Schomberg when he arrived in Bangor in 1689. He was followed by his brother Henry, and then by yet another Hugh, the Fourth Earl, a son of Henry. When he died, his younger brother Thomas became the fifth and last earl. This was the man who married the renowned Marie Angélique de la Cherois, a Lisburn Huguenot.

The Delacherois family

During the sixteenth century the French followers of the teachings of Calvin and Knox became known as Huguenots. They suffered considerable persecution until the 1598 Edict of Nantes gave them the right to live freely in France as a minority faith. When King Louis XIV revoked this 'perpetual and irrevocable' edict in 1685, the persecution that followed drove Huguenots out of France in all directions.

About ten thousand of these refugees settled in Ireland. Amongst them were three de la Cherois brothers, who had come with the French Huguenot regiment in William III's army.[2] Nicholas de la Cherois was a major who distinguished himself at the Battle of the Boyne; Daniel was a captain, and Boisgonval a lieutenant who was killed in the fighting in Dungannon.

Louis Crommelin, from St. Quentin in Picardy, was another notable Huguenot refugee. Like the de la Cherois brothers, he invested in the thriving linen industry in the Lagan Valley. As the industry grew, Crommelin and the Lisburn-based de la Cherois family prospered.[3]

In 1700, Daniel de la Cherois had a daughter, Marie Angélique.[4] Twenty-five years later, after a brief first marriage to a London merchant named Philip Grueber, this vivacious lady married Thomas Montgomery, the Fifth Earl of Mount-Alexander. This was the archetypal union between good blood and money, and the marriage endured until Montgomery's death in 1757. When Marie Angélique died in 1771, she bequeathed the former Montgomery estates around Donaghadee to Daniel Delacherois, the son of her Hilden cousin Samuel.

A small but fine eighteenth century mansion known as the Manor House stands near the top end of High Street in Donaghadee. It is still occupied by

Portrait thought to be of Hugh Montgomery, Second Earl of Mount Alexander, who led the county's Williamites in 1689. (Day family)

La belle Marie Angélique Delacherois, a remarkable lady, who charmed all who knew her. (Day Family)

members of the Delacherois family.

A few yards further up the hill lies an older and more enigmatic dwelling called Rosebank House. It was erected in the seventeenth century,[5] and can make a strong claim to have been Donaghadee's original, seventeenth century Manor House. It is handsome and imposing. It has a commanding view of the harbour. It is marked as the largest house in the town on an eighteenth century map.[6] It has a fresh water spring in its cellar; and there is evidence of fortifications of the kind that a lord of the manor would have demanded in those turbulent days.

There is ample evidence that there was a Manor House in Donaghadee prior

to Daniel Delacherois' arrival in 1771.[7] But for reasons unknown – maybe the house was too unfashionable, maybe its site was too exposed – Delacherois did not wish to live in it, and so a new house was commissioned in Donaghadee.

This house, the modern Manor House, would appear to have been completed by 1780,[8] for it is shown in a map of Donaghadee that is generally agreed to have been drawn by Daniel Delacherois in that year. The map also shows that major building works were then underway, including the cutting of the appropriately named New Street.[9] Delacherois died childless in 1790,[10] before his plans for a Market House in New Street could be brought to fruition,[11] having made a determined and imaginative effort to aggrandize the town.

Marie Angélique's other beneficiaries were the children of Madeleine Delacherois, the wife of Daniel Crommelin.[12] Their youngest son, De La Cherois Crommelin, married Elizabeth Piers and they had a daughter, Mary Angelica. In 1785, she married the Rev. Dr. Francis Hutchinson, who served as

Rosebank House, which may have been the Montgomery Manor House until the death of Marie Angélique, Countess of Mount Alexander.

The Manor House, home of the Delacherois family since the 1770s. (Robert Neill Collection)

rector of Donaghadee from 1787-1814. They had one daughter, named Elizabeth after her grandmother. This girl married George Leslie, her near neighbour in Rosebank. He was the son of Edmund Leslie, the Archdeacon of Down. Their daughter Ellen later married another Daniel Delacherois who was the squire of the town until 1905.

This marriage produced a son named George, and he in turn had two daughters. Many Donaghadee readers will know these redoubtable ladies as Mrs Jacqueline Day and the late Mrs Georgina Stone. The latter died childless in 2002, but Mrs Day has two daughters, Angélique and Jacqueline, and a son, Nicholas. The last-named currently resides in Donaghadee's Manor House with his wife Heather and family.

'A town whose star has fallen'
During the reign of William IV, the momentous decision was made to map the entire island of Ireland. Skilled map-makers from the army's department of ordnance undertook the work. Their maps were accompanied by memoirs, in which everything considered important or interesting was written down.

The Memoirs for the Parish of Donaghadee were completed between 1832-37 by Lieutenant Henry Tucker and M.M. Kertland. They tell us much about

The Delacherois folly stands sentinel over Moat Street. (Elizabeth Taggart)

the town and its environs. We learn, for instance, that there were then 650 houses in Donaghadee, some 430 of which were single-storied. Only 160 houses were thatched, the remainder being roofed with the cheaper and better Tullycavey and Ballygrainey slate.

We learn that Donaghadee possessed 'a greater degree of cleanliness than is usual in Ireland'. We are told that there were just three policemen in the town, a number considered, 'quite sufficient owing to the very peaceable and quiet

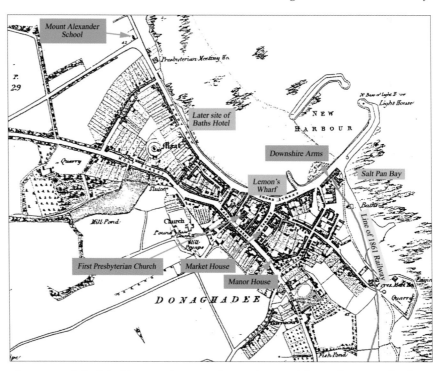

Mount Alexander School

Later site of Baths Hotel

Downshire Arms

Salt Pan Bay

Lemon's Wharf

First Presbyterian Church

Market House

Manor House

Donaghadee in 1834.

character of the inhabitants who are sober and peaceable, and not much given to amusement'. This was possibly because 'no illicit distillation whatever is carried on.' Kertland also refers to the Copeland Islands, stating that are the property of David Ker of Portavo, and remarking that:

There is no coastguard station on the island. An attempt was made to establish one some time ago, but it met with effectual opposition from Mr Ker.[13]

Ker went further, insisting that no coastguard vessel should be moored anywhere near the islands. With a shrug of the shoulders, Kertland adds that occasional surveillance from Donaghadee cannot prevent the smuggling of tobacco, rum and brandy into the islands in the hours of darkness. Perhaps this is why Donaghadee had no need of pot-stills.

Censuses arrived at around the same time as the Ordnance Survey, becoming increasingly detailed and reliable as the decades passed. The 1871 census for example, shows 2,226 people living in the town of Donaghadee. It had a youthful population; of its 874 males, 380 (or 43%) were under twenty years old. The sea, in its various guises, remained the town's economic mainstay. Most of its menfolk were seamen of one hue or another, and in 1871 we read that seventeen fishermen and a staggering ninety coastguards lived in the town.

Eighty-four men were employed as general labourers, and thirty-six described themselves as either farmers or farm labourers. Thirty-seven are recorded as shopkeepers, eleven of whom were butchers, and sixteen grocers. Donaghadee boasted six schoolmasters, four innkeepers, nine carpenters, three bricklayers, six painters/glaziers, four masons and an amazing twenty-four shoemakers.[14] The High Street-New Street axis formed the commercial centre of the town.

Street directories also offer us some choice tit-bits. The 1863 Belfast and Ulster Street Directory is particularly valuable because it was published at a time of great change. Donaghadee had recently experienced the closure of the packet route and the completion of the railway. The directory reflects this, showing us a town that is aligning itself away from its picturesque, semi-retired harbour and towards the new railway.

The string of hotels on the Parade now owed their existence not to the port but to the railway. Daniel Delacherois had even been obliged to raze his popular Sea Baths Hotel at Saltpan Bay because it was on the best line for the railway.[15] Delacherois and his new partner, Donaghadee's brick and tile merchant, James Duffy, received sufficient compensation to open the new Ulster Baths Hotel on the Parade in 1872.

Across the Parade we see mentioned the Railway, the Eagle, the Commercial and Arthur's Hotels. All lay between New Street and the station entrance. The directory praises the town's pleasant appearance, and admires its beaches, baths, and splendid harbour. Surprisingly, just three of the businesses in the small commercial heart of Donaghadee are public houses, Hugh Heron's and Robert Walker's in New Street, and Mary Connolly's in High Street. The smaller taverns and spirit grocers lie in the quieter, more residential streets of the town – i.e. where their local customers lived.[16]

Between 1863, and the publication of Bassett's County Down Directory in 1885, the size of the town changed little.[17] Bassett described Donaghadee as lying between the harbour on the east coast and the wonderfully named Cat Loanin[18] (later Northfield) on the west; and between Clayhole Row (now Killaughey Road) to the south, and Bullock Row (now East Street) on its north

New Road doorway. In the late nineteenth century the Delacherois family gentrified the northern part of the town. (Elizabeth Taggart)

The Promenade, Donaghadee

Cabbies gather at the station under the watchful eye of the law. (Robert Neill Collection)

side. Outside the town, Erin Lodge, now smothered by the Rosepark development, stood alone in its own fine grounds.

Bassett recorded eighteen grocers' shops in the town, suggesting a relatively comfortable standard of living. This small rise in numbers also implies that the town had to some extent 'bounced back' from the loss of the packet service and found a new stability. But Bassett also described Donaghadee as 'a town whose star has fallen'. He is right to suggest that the loss of the steam packet service was a devastating blow, but his guide makes clear that the harbour was far from disused. Its thirty yawls regularly brought in fresh whitefish, eels, lobsters and cod. The South Pier was busy with coal schooners from Whitehaven, unloading into railway wagons that took their cargoes on to Newtownards and Comber.

The Royal Irish Constabulary (RIC) kept order, and police barracks appear at different times at different locations. In the 1860s, a barrack can be identified on the corner of Church Lane and High Street. A little later, one appears in

Rathmore Terrace on the corner of Union Street and Moat Street. During the Great War, the RIC can be found at 4 Shore Street, next door to an ice-cream parlour owned by an Enrico Caproni. Since the 1930s, Donaghadee's police have been based in the Rippingham-designed RUC building on the Millisle Road.

During the nineteenth century, Donaghadee's streets differed little from those of the approaching country roads in that they had a mixture of stones, clay and horse manure as their topcoat. When New Street was cut in the early 1780s, it would have had a similar surface. Vulnerable stretches may have been paved with square-setts, or the less pedestrian-friendly 'kidney-pavers'. Donaghadee's dusty (or muddy) outer streets were no better or worse than those of any Victorian town. And like these towns, it lacked amenities such as electricity, street lighting, or dustbins.[19]

As the new century dawned, an anonymous Donaghadee correspondent described how the town's water came from a scatter of hand-pumps, and that few houses had bathrooms or flush lavatories. Some, he says, did not even have their own outside privy, and were forced to share. He asked how the 1898 Towns' Improvement Act might assist what he called the 'most backward town in Ireland', and called for street lighting, declaring that its absence was responsible for much immorality.[20]

The anonymous letter writer added that the lack of sanitation and piped water made Donaghadee 'ripe for any dreadful disease under the sun'. There had been such epidemics in the past. In the Parish Church Register we read that between July-September 1832, the rector buried fifty-three Donaghadee victims of cholera.[21] The only answer to this, the correspondent claimed, was to create an Urban Council as soon as possible. The town had only to wait until 1908.[22]

Armed RIC man. Between three and six police officers were typically stationed in the town.

8 Employers and employed

Two chandlers' tales

All ports need ships' carpenters, sail-makers, chandlers, rope-makers, dockers and stevedores. Donaghadee was well provided for in each of these departments. Its most successful entrepreneur in the days of sail was a ship-owner and chandler called James Lemon, the man James Arbuckle had described in 1796 as a 'foolish fellow.' James was the son of William Lemon, a coastguard officer from Ballyhalbert. As a young man, James had become Seneschal, or estate manager, of the Delacherois properties.[1] By the 1790s, as we have seen, he had fallen foul of the establishment figures in the town because of his staunch Presbyterianism and his sympathy with the United Irishmen.

After the Rebellion, Lemon expanded his business on the Parade, operating and fitting-out his own ships and supplying other companies' ships. Granny's Corner is still known to many as Lemon's Wharf. By the late 1830s Lemon had moved his ships' chandlery premises to Hanover Quay in Belfast, and bought a ropeworks in Ballymacarrett.[2]

Lemon's 'heir' in Donaghadee was a James Tedford, who from 1843 onwards operated as a ship owner, coal and salt dealer, and ironmonger in New Street, possibly after having taken over Lemon's property when he left it.[3] Local tradition has always had it that Tedford's premises were on the corner of New Street and the Parade, from where he could keep a watchful eye on the harbour from which he made his money.[4]

Tedford's business moved to Belfast in 1851 – to premises right beside those of James Lemon! Today, both these old names have gone, but Tedford's building is still standing, as a smart restaurant, on what is now called Donegall Quay. Tedford and Lemon knew one another well, and Tedford's move to Belfast was probably spurred by the knowledge of how well his mentor was doing, but whether Tedford came as a colleague or a rival isn't known.

For many years Lemon's firm, later run by his sons, was the bigger, but in time Tedford's enterprise prevailed. With its date-stone, sail lofts and distinctive navy-blue pulley block on its sky-blue frontage, Tedford's became a well-known symbol of Belfast's maritime trade.

The embroidery boom

Lemon and Tedford would have employed many local men, and the activities listed above would have occasioned jobs for many others. But until 1800, there was little employment for women outside of domestic service or the spinning of yarn. The new century changed everything. In 1837, a contemporary visitor to Donaghadee noted that:

The women and girls are chiefly employed at a kind of ornamental needlework called flowering, which consists of delineating flowers and other objects upon a reticulated medium, through the instrumentality of a needle and thread. [5]

The embroidering of white muslin and light linen lawn fabrics had become commonplace in the Ards. Such embroidery was known as tambour work, or in some places 'sprigging' or 'spoking'.

Towards the end of the eighteenth century, machine spinning had wiped out hand spinning as a cottage industry in Scotland and Ulster, and left thousands in need of employment. Some enterprising men in Glasgow began to farm out pieces of cotton or linen for skilled women to embroider. Designs were carved on wooden cylinders, which were rolled onto the cloth as a pattern for overstitching. The sewers stretched the cloth taut on a frame known as a tambour frame,[6] and then embroidered it in decorative patterns, in designs based on leaves and flowers. The work was sometimes done indoors, but was more often conducted in the better light outside the stitchers' front doors.

This cottage industry began in Ayrshire, but demand grew, and it was not long before the trade was in search of fresh labour. In 1813, a Lisburn muslin manufacturer called George Duncan brought a Scotswoman over to teach local women and girls the art of tambouring.[7] The craft had arrived in Ireland.

Ulster people were of course no strangers to flax. It had long been grown in the Ards, and some of its wee blue blossoms even decorated fields near

A new set of sails, or dinner for two? James Tedford opened his ships' chandlery business in these well-known premises by the River Lagan in 1851, after outgrowing Donaghadee.

Sprigging or flowering. A grandmother and grand-daughter embroider in the better light outdoors.

Donaghadee. Flax had been spun and woven here too,[8] and until the 1990s the stark ruins of Moore's flax-mill could still be seen by the High Bangor Road. By 1820, sprigging had taken root in the Ards. It was not long before the siren-call of the Scottish embroidery agents called many more to this new cottage trade.

A Dublin man named John Cochrane set up an agency for embroidery work in Donaghadee, then handier to Ayrshire than to Belfast. By 1824, John Cochrane & Sons were flourishing.[9] Before long, Cochrane had become the best and cheapest dealer of sewed muslins in the United Kingdom.[10] As the production of lightweight linens expanded, the spokers took to embroidering these fabrics too.

High Street and Shore Street were soon awash with agencies, which distributed cloth made in Glasgow across the cabins and cottages of north Down, collecting the finished work a week or so later.

By 1846, sprigging, or spoking, had become big business, with agencies for Glasgow embroidery houses operating in most towns in the north of Ireland. Embroidery had become big business. Belfast had thirty-one muslin manufactories. Seventeen more firms made 'sewed muslin.' By the mid-

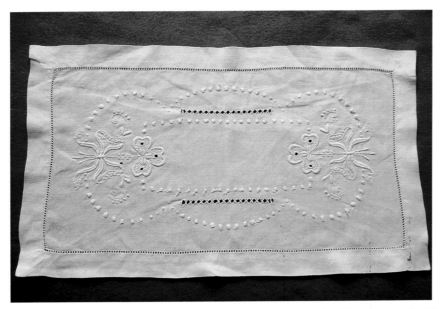

A century-old piece of hand-sprigging from the Ards. This subtle, 'white on white' work was esteemed the world over.

century, about 200,000 Ulsterwomen were engaged in embroidery, almost half of them in County Down.[11]

Donaghadee become the *entrepôt* for an amazingly elaborate putting-out system that was carried out all over the county. Newtownards was an equally important player. Thirty-one muslin manufactories operated in the town, twenty of them making and preparing cloth for embroidery. Lisburn, by contrast, had eleven muslin manufacturers, but no embroidery agents. Towns as far west as Raphoe also had local agencies.[12]

By the 1860s, although Donaghadee had lost its prime position, it remained an important factoring centre. Men like William Brown in High Street, Michael Robinson in Moat Street, James Allan and John McMeekin in New Street, and Eliza Purdy and Mary Martin on the Parade, represented major Glasgow companies like John Cochrane, Robert, Samuel and Thomas Brown, Hay and Bartholomew, Sharpe and Co., and William Weir Jun. & Co. The postmaster, John McGowan, operated a part-time agency, and John Jamison ran a sewing 'factory' on Shore Street.[13]

So many thousands of pieces of this 'white on white' work found their way into fashionable drawing rooms, kitchens and bedrooms in Europe and

Schooners, c. 1910. (Robert Neill Collection)

America that flowering became better known than lace. Within a fifteen-mile semi-circle round Donaghadee, up to fifteen thousand workers embroidered cloth for christening robes, ladies' caps and collars. Suitably sized pieces became napkins, pillow-cases, antimacassars, and runners for sideboards and tables. The finished produce was then shipped from Donaghadee to Glasgow, where it was often marketed as Scotch work!

Thanks to her numerous other duties and the poor light, the woman of the house rarely did more than ten hours of sewing in a winter week, and perhaps twenty or thirty in summer. Perched on stiff bentwood chairs, women sat with their sewing, trying to catch as many hours of daylight as possible before their fingers numbed with the cold. Sewing and embroidery were added to the school curriculum.

The piece-work wages of the embroiderers varied from one shilling and sixpence a week for the less-skilful children and the stiff-fingered grannies, to four shillings a week for the most able stitchers. In Scotland, payments could be twice this, a differential the agencies justified by claiming that much Ulster 'white work' came back to Scotland besmirched with smoke and grease, or smelling of peat-reek and bacon. Sullied pieces had to be soaked, bleached and dried on a green before they were considered pristine enough for sale.[14]

Ardsmen had always plied their labour on the sea and in the fields. Now their wives, sisters and daughters acquired their own sources of income. Many thousands spent their lifetimes flowering cotton, muslin and linen, toiling from the age of six until their hands or their eyesight wore out. Their earnings enabled them to procure extras for their families, and to make their cottages a little more comfortable. It brought women a measure of economic independence. In some households the wage meant even more. One stitcher believed that 'without it we might die for want of food.'[15] During the Great Famine, various Glasgow embroidery houses contributed between £10 and £25 to the fund set up by the Visiting Committee of the Newtownards Workhouse.[16]

Embroidery provided something of a lifeline during these terrible years, but in 1857 a financial crisis in the United States halved prices for embroidery.[17] Poorer people could now afford flowered work, and what had once been fashionable suddenly became outmoded. Difficulties with the cotton supply during the American Civil dealt another blow to the embroidery trade.

But flowering remained important. In 1871, 427 or 32% of the 1,352 women and girls living in town of Donaghadee held textile-related jobs, 230 of them in embroidery.[18] Gradually, however, machine work replaced hand work, until by the 1920s, commercial hand embroidery, once the district's mainstay, had virtually disappeared.

9 Churches and schools

From St. Patrick to John Wesley

House of God? The tower of Donaghadee Parish Church was fashioned from a late medieval tower house. The dwelling's first-floor fireplaces and defensive arrow loops remain, but nothing is now known about its occupants.

According to local tradition, on his arrival in Ireland, St. Patrick landed not in Saul but in the townland of Templepatrick, a mile out of Donaghadee. At the south end of Ballyvester beach lies a stone containing 'St. Patrick's Footprints', holes the shape and size of human feet. This rock is said to mark the spot where the saint set foot in Ireland.

Seven hundred years after Patrick, the Normans built a stone church in Donaghadee.[1] By the time Hugh Montgomery arrived in 1606, this had fallen into ruins, so in 1626 he erected a new house of worship on the site of the present parish church, pressing the remains of a fifteenth or sixteenth century tower house into service as its tower.[2] The present tower was added in 1833, with the west vestry being built later. The Delacherois vault was constructed beneath the west transept in 1866.[3] The knowledge that many sarcophagi lie therein has caused this raised area to be called 'Mount Misery' ever since. The great bell was donated in 1877, the church was greatly enlarged in 1881, and the clock was added in 1892.

Officially, Montgomery's church was Anglican. But his Presbyterian tenants stuck stubbornly to the articles of faith that they had learned in their Ayrshire kirks, and its early ministers, such as Rev. Nevin and the Rev. Andrew Stewart, were in practice non-conformist.[4] In the 1660s, this ambiguity ceased to be tolerated. Sixty-one Presbyterian ministers in the new Ulster colony, including Donaghadee's Andrew Stewart, were ejected from their parishes for refusing to conform to the episcopal church.

The Dissenters, who were the great majority in the community, now erected a simple place of worship, traditionally located just out of the town at Killaughey. It was referred to as the 'Sod Church', as its walls were constructed of earthen sods. An eighteenth diary relates a cautionary tale about this structure.

On the afternoon of Saturday June 8th 1706, a young man called James Allen, the son of Francis Allen the postmaster (whom we met in chapter two), fired his musket at a bird on the church roof. A piece of wadding landed on the thatch and set it on fire, but the blaze was put out before it could consume the building.[5]

Some years after this drama, the Presbyterians of Donaghadee built a more substantial church at the south end of the town. Its first minister was the Rev. William Warnock, who began his ministry there in 1747.[6] The church was at the far end of what became Meetinghouse Street, near what is now the Marina.[7] In 1764, 95% of the parish's population of 1,948 was Presbyterian.[8]

Most of this number worshipped here until 1819, when a row about the morals of their pastor, the Reverend William Skelly, split the congregation.[9] Skelly had arrived in 1812. A few years later he was accused of behaving improperly. In 1819, the division became a breach, and what had been a harmonious congregation for two centuries became two separate churches as Skelly's loyal supporters would not remain within the church that had shunned him. In 1821 Skelly was deposed by the General Synod, and for a time he and his reduced congregation found temporary accommodation.

Down but not out, Skelly and his followers built a new church on Shore Street, beside Daniel Saul's ropeworks (now Shore Street Green).[10] There is a local tradition that, outside his own loyal following, their pastor's unpopularity prevented the congregation from obtaining a building site inside the town. Skelly's solution was to buy a plot on the rocky foreshore and build a church 'outwith' Donaghadee. It cost £600, and by 1822 up to 450 subscribers were holding services there.[11] In 1856, the General Synod bought Shore Street Church for £200, and restored Skelly and the breakaway congregation to the fold.[12] Skelly lived in a manse opposite East Street until his death in 1857. In one of history's pithier ironies, this Calvinist manse would eventually become the Moat Inn.

The major part of the old congregation had meanwhile found a prime site in High Street, where they built a new place of worship. Retaining the name of First Donaghadee, they strove to erect a larger church than Skelly's. The impressive classical lines of First Donaghadee appeared in 1824. The church building cost £815 and could accommodate 500 worshippers.[13] Its first preacher was the Rev. John McAuley, who ministered in Donaghadee for over half a century.

The church's prominent position in High Street was quite deliberate, the site being chosen because it was right in the heart of Donaghadee, beside the town's only hotel.[14] The distance between the building fronts at both ends of High Street is about thirty-five feet; but about half way along it, the street broadens to a width of about fifty feet. This 'bulge' marks the point at which the old roads from Newtownards, Bangor and the peninsula met. It is also likely to have been the town's market place until the erection of the Market House in New Street in 1819.

The founder of Methodism, John Wesley, often came to Ireland. Some accounts say that he made as many as forty journeys between 1747-91, some of them through Donaghadee, although Wesley's meticulous journals are infuriatingly coy about his time in the town.

Donaghadee Methodists are more inclined to regard a determined lady called Mary Carey as their 'founding father'. In around 1790, some Belfast adherents of Wesley's had converted her to Methodism. Initially, she walked to

Martyr's memorial? Shore Street Presbyterian Church. (Elizabeth Taggart)

Classical grace. First Presbyterian Church, built 1824. (Elizabeth Taggart)

worship in Belfast, but in time she arranged for services to be held in Donaghadee's corn-kiln.[15]

A small number of Wesleyans worshipped there for twenty years, until a well-connected lady called Mrs Smith joined the congregation. She begged her kinsman Daniel Delacherois for a site near the kiln, and convinced a Mrs Gayer from Derriaghy near Lisburn to give her five guineas.[16] By 1813, thirty guineas had been donated – a sufficient sum to allow a house of worship to be built on the present church site.

The dreadful cholera outbreak of 1832 provoked such a fear of death that many converted to Methodism in the decades following.[17] As the church grew, a Sunday School, and later a National School were accommodated on the continually improving premises. A new church was erected in 1849, and an almost complete re-build was completed in 1909 on the original site.[18]

Catholicism was also growing. By the 1830s, Catholic numbers were sufficient to allow masses to be held locally. Eventually, with the support of local people and the financial assistance of the other churches in the town, the Catholics acquired the funds to build a church near the foot of High Street. In time the congregation moved to a new church on the Millisle Road, where it continues to worship. Only the facade and the 1845 datestone of the original church remain.

This pre-1909 view of Donaghadee from the Parish Church tower shows First Presbyterian (centre r), St. Comgall's (bottom r) and the Methodist Church, without its cupola (bottom left). (Robert Neill Collection)

Graveyard gleanings

Until the opening of the new cemetery at Ballyvester in 1947, the Church of Ireland graveyard was the town's only burying place. This venerable burial ground contains at least a thousand marked graves, and over six hundred headstones which have had their inscriptions recorded.[19] These commemorate everyone from the members of the knightly Delacherois family, lying resplendent in their vault, through soldiers, sailors, coastguards, fishermen, centenarians, clergymen of all faiths, and identified and unknown drowned people, to anonymous babies.[20]

The oldest stone in the churchyard is a memorial to a William Scott, mariner, dated December 20th 1660. Near it, by the path on the east side of the church, stands another sandstone monument which for many years hid its face in the earth, having been recycled by another family. Its obverse face commemorates a Jean Mackgwear, who 'lived wel and died wel' until her death in 1660,[21] something anyone might wish for. Inside the church are numerous fine memorials. One of the most intriguing is a bronze plaque commemorating a very special man.

William David Kenny was the son of John Joseph Kenny, an RIC constable from County Monaghan, and his wife Miriam from Antrim. While his father was stationed in Donaghadee, William was a pupil in the Admiral Leslie School, where he gained a scholarship to Mountjoy School in Dublin. As a young man William was a noted athlete, winning inter-provincial rugby caps for Leinster. When the Great War broke out the Donaghadee man joined the Indian Army, and by 1918 he was serving with the 4/39th Royal Garwhal Rifles at Kot-Kai on the Afghanistan-India frontier.

This war did not stop with the Armistice. Early in 1920, William and a handful of his men held a redoubt against massed Mahsuds for over four hours while the rest of his regiment and their wounded were evacuated. Lieutenant Kenny and all his men were killed, and he was posthumously awarded the Victoria Cross for conspicuous valour.[22] The citizens of Donaghadee were so proud of their hero that they altered the dates of the First World War on their war memorial to 1914-20 to encompass this action, thus setting it in a slightly less accurate, but in some ways truer, context.

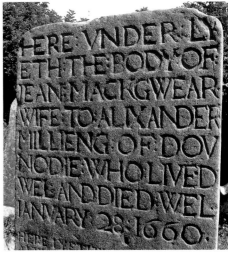

Lived well, died well, and left a good looking headstone. Jean Mackgwear's memorial in Donaghadee Churchyard.

Kenny's last stand at Kot Kai, by Fred Roe, from an old newspaper cutting.

Donaghadee's National Schools

The first known school in Donaghadee was the Mount Alexander, a private school founded in 1771 with money bequeathed by Marie Angélique Delacherois, supplemented by a gift from Mr Semphill, two of the prominent Donaghadee citizens that James Boswell had dined with two years before. It was latterly sited at the foot of New Road. [23]

Its sister school was the Admiral Leslie Free School. The appellation 'sister' is appropriate, not only because both were Church of Ireland schools, but because Mount Alexander had been set up exclusively for boys, and the Admiral Leslie, completed in 1872, was for girls. The school building stands proudly on the corner of Manor Street and Millisle Road. It is now the town's Baptist church.

This school was also founded by a woman, Mrs Martha Leslie of Rosebank House, who named it after her late husband, Rear-Admiral Samuel Leslie.[24] A

Not a church but a temple of learning. The Admiral Leslie School.

In 1840, this atmospheric ruin was the brand new Bow Lane National School.

portion of her bequest was invested so that thirty of the neediest young girls in the town could receive a free education. There was also funding for blue surplices for the 'free' pupils to wear to protect their clothes, and of course publicly identify them in the usual Victorian way. All the other pupils had to pay to learn, and on Monday mornings the children would each have carried their family's contribution of a penny towards the schoolteacher's wages.

In 1831, the National Schools scheme was established in an attempt to loosen the churches' grip on education. Successful applicants received National School status, which meant that they were provided with books and equipment, and some help with their teachers' salaries. Donaghadee's first National School opened in 1839 – the 209th in Ireland. It did not last long, and almost nothing is known of it today, although it is probably the school still recalled by the name Schoolhouse Brae.

It was not long before other schools followed. Bow Lane became a National School in 1840. The school included an apartment for the schoolmistress, and was entered from the yard behind the Market House in New Street. The neat building that once housed this early National School is now a stark and ruinous shell.

Notwithstanding the government's best intentions, most schools applying for grant aid remained closely attached to their founder churches. First Presbyterian soon had its National School (located in what is now called the Curragh Room); the Methodists had their school, operating in what today is the Wesley Hall, and by 1861 Shore Street had its own school, in a building that has only recently disappeared amidst church renovations. The Mount Alexander and the Admiral Leslie schools held out from joining, but finally succumbed in 1888.

The Rev. William Skelly's 1861 application for grant aid for the Shore Street school is a wonderful indicator of what facilities were like at the time. Skelly boasted that his new school was built on the latest principles, that it had a *ceiling* and that its floor was made of *wooden boards*. Not content with these luxuries it also had 'two privies in the rere – *properly separated*, and so arranged that the nuisance is carried away by the rain water falling on the roof.' The clear implication is that the italicised features were superior to those in some existing schools nearby.

That they were so is borne out by the inspector's report on First Donaghadee's school in 1870. It recounts a long dispute between the church and the National Board about whether Board money would be better spent on schoolbooks, or in culverting the open sewer that drained the school's privies across the Parade and into the sea. A difficult choice indeed! By one of history's ironies this building now serves as the town's public toilets.

Country folk wanted schools too. There is documentary evidence of thirty-two schools operating, although not all at once, in the Donaghadee parish area during the nineteenth century. Twenty-one of these were established before 1850.[25]

Ballywilliam had its own school, the foundations of which are now totally invisible beneath the grassy foreshore near Barnhill. Old National School buildings still stand at Millisle, Grangee, Carrowdore, Cottown, Woburn, Killaughey and Ballyvester – the first is now a church and the remainder are private dwelling houses. Nearby, although technically in Bangor parish, were schools at the Cottown and (at two separate times, as needed) on the Great Copeland Island.

The story of Ballyvester National School, a mile or so to the west of Donaghadee, shows how a community could raise the money to build their children a school. The present school was built in 1906, but the original schoolhouse lies just across the Ballyvester Road, in what is now a dwelling

This datestone, commemorating the foundation of Ballyvester School in 1842, came to light during a recent renovation of the old school building.

house. This older building still displays an intriguing 1842 datestone above its door. In 1976, before this inscription was uncovered, a tiny notebook was shown to the author. It had been discovered by the Public Record Office in a huge pile of papers rescued from a Belfast merchant's.[26] The book told a wonderful tale.

In 1840, at the time when education was fast-growing in the town of Donaghadee, the Presbyterians of Ballyvester were determined that their children would have a new school. A building fund was opened. Contributions ranged from the proverbial widow's mite to donations from Glasgow embroidery merchants. The local builders itemised every piece of work necessary, right down to nails, and even 'to drawing sand – 6d.' Their total came to £35. The money was raised. But then the treasurer pointed out that they would need £39.

The local ministers immediately rallied to the cause and preached some outdoor sermons, with the collections going to the school fund. The shortfall was soon made up, and the school opened, to everyone's satisfaction, in the summer of 1842. It has flourished ever since, first as a community school, then under the National Board, then as a Public Elementary, and now as a fine Primary School – with only one change of premises in almost two centuries.

In 1931, the Bishop of Down and Connor asked Downpatrick Convent to open a primary school in Donaghadee, mainly for Catholic children. In 1932, St. Anne's Convent School was opened in High Street, with thirty pupils.

The Mount Alexander and Admiral Leslie Free Schools eventually went co-educational. The Donaghadee schools flourished during the nineteenth century, each in its separate way, and according to the inspectors' reports, they produced young adults with a noticeably higher level of education than in many parts of Ireland.

After the Second World War, the aging National Schools, then known as Public Elementaries, were replaced by a new primary school on Northfield in 1954. In 1956 this was supplemented by what was then a state-of-the-art secondary school – now Donaghadee High School. In 1962, a brand new St. Anne's School was built in the grounds of the Shandon Presbytery House.

These three Donaghadee schools, along with nearby Ballyvester Primary continue to serve the changing needs of the community after the example set by their predecessors, even if they would be almost unrecognisable to a founder-pupil of Mount Alexander Endowed School, way back in 1771.

10 Donaghadee's river

A river journey

Many people will be surprised to hear that Donaghadee has a river. Truth to tell, it is little more than a stream, but when the district's earliest inhabitants settled at its mouth, the fresh water it provided sustained their lives. For centuries its flow was crucial to the development of the town. Today it is little more than an open sewer, and it would be a brave person indeed who would drink its water.

This little river rises four miles inland in Ballyhay townland, then zig-zags its way as an open stream to the edge of the all-weather hockey pitch, from where it continues in a culvert to the back of the parish church. From here, the subterranean 'burn' flows along the side of the Shilling Hill, and then down Church Lane. This part of the burn was open until the 1960s, passing under a little bridge at the gateway to the private gardens of the Delacherois family, now the gardens of Northfield House.

From this now-bricked-up doorway, a secluded walkway led to the gate opposite the Manor House. On the opposite side of Church Lane, the 'walks' continued through trees to the Manor Farm. This quiet lane was occasionally opened for the town's citizens to enjoy, but more often gave members of the Delacherois family privacy as they strolled to and from their home, or went to church. The burn courses from the gateway behind the Chapel, under the buildings on the south side of High Street, to Bridge Street and into the sea.

It has largely followed the same course since the last Ice Age. On the shore the first Mesolithic explorers would have found a rich supply of fish and shellfish. There would have been roots, nuts and berries to eat, and animals to

The gateway to the 'walks' that led to the Manor Farm. (Elizabeth Taggart)

be trapped. But unlike other places with similar food sources, this site had an inexhaustible supply of fresh water. This would probably have been enough to convince some of them to settle.

In time, people began to keep animals and plant crops. During the Bronze Age they boiled meat in huge cooking pits at Ballycroghan, using the water from the nearby stream and heated stones.[1] The river which runs through Donaghadee may have had its pits too.

When Montgomery's colonists arrived in 1606, they sank wells to obtain their drinking water, rather than use the river's sometimes suspect supply. But this did not render Donaghadee's river redundant. In the eighteenth century its waters were again prized, this time as a source of power.

By 1835, the parish of Donaghadee had acquired a number of mills. Seven were windmills – four of which stood in the townland of Ballycopeland.[2] These flamboyant structures were complemented by a smaller number of watermills. The Carmichael family ran three in Donaghadee and Millisle, and these somewhat more reliable concerns milled the bulk of the parish's corn and flax.

The breast for Donaghadee's mill-dam lay where the British Legion Hall stands today. The Dam Field once contained a reservoir roughly three acres in extent, which was capable of holding between two and three million gallons of water. In 1861, the Belfast and County Down Railway Company so coveted its fresh water that they gave the Carmichael family free travel on their trains in exchange for the right to pipe supplies of it down to Donaghadee station for their locomotives.

As well as being handy for industrial purposes, the mill-pond made a great swimming hole for hot and sweaty children during the summer months. In the autumn its water was needed to drive the mill's fourteen-foot wheel.

The dam water reached the mill wheel via a millrace. This ran past Andrew Ringland's blacksmith's forge,[3] across Church Place, under the wall beside Francis Allen's gates, then along the side of the graveyard and under its back footpath to the mill in Church Lane, now gone.[4] Its stone-flagged channel lay dry for most of the year, but when the great sluice gate was opened for the first milling, a raging torrent cascaded down the race, or leet, and set the big wheel turning. When harvest finished the sluice was closed and the water resumed its course.

The stream's course dictated the location of another essential amenity in the town. This was the animal pound, still visible at the rear of the parish churchyard, where impounded animals were kept. It was not created for the welfare of the animals, but in order to prevent unscrupulous owners from allowing their livestock to 'graze the lazy acre', or eat their neighbours' grass.

Anyone who had a large animal impounded could secure its release within a period of three days upon payment of a stiff fine. The tariff for a horse, mare, mule, ass, or horned beast was 6d, and a calf, lamb, goat or pig, a rather less painful 2d. The impounded animals got their water for free, but they were charged for the fodder they ate whilst impounded.[5] The river's fresh water must have sustained many an abandoned animal until its owner scraped up the pennies needed to release it.

Nearby, where the Courtyard apartments now stand, John Gibson had a butcher's shop, but one that was a little different. For sound topographical reasons, Gibson's also served as the town's slaughter house and skinners' yard. All the cattle, sheep and pigs destined for the table were taken to Mr Gibson's and properly dispatched. Whilst still warm, the bodies were skinned and gutted, and had their unappetising parts removed. Each of the other butchers in the town would then bring his cart to Church Lane, and buy whatever carcases he needed.

The Gibsons then had to dispose of the blood and unwanted flesh – and where better than directly into the Donaghadee River. By clever design, the

Northern Ireland's only working windmill. In the nineteenth century the famous Ballycopeland Windmill was one of seven in the parish.

drains in Gibson's yard lay directly over the stream – the local rats must have had a field day![6]

When the hides were clean and 'green', they were carried the ten yards across Church Lane to the town's tanyard, which was replete with pits full of the dyes and acids necessary for its work. The tanyard's waste liquids were probably disposed of in the same way as those of the skinners. This yard later became McConkey's Court. After the tanyard pits were filled in, Robert McConkey had twelve houses built there in about 1900.

The culvert finally opened at 5 High Street. From here, the burn ran *au naturelle* along the south-east side of Bridge Street, emptying into the sea under the little bridge on the Parade that gave the street its name. On the shore side of the sea wall one may still see the arch of this bridge. In the mid-1980s, the stream was re-routed to reach the foreshore near the war memorial.

Old Donaghadee town

John Bennett's yard stood directly opposite the tanyard. John built Bennett's Avenue, much of Stellenbosch Avenue, and many other houses in Donaghadee. In 1976, in his living room in Hunter's Lane, he spoke about the town he loved so well.[7] This transcription of his words cannot hope to convey his rich,

'Are ye comin' for a pint?' The legendary Grace Neill's bar. (Elizabeth Taggart)

unaffected, Ulster-Scots baritone, but it nonetheless opens a fascinating window onto the past.

'Ah was born in the Sanny Raw', John began, 'up the shore there – ye know where McKibben's, the agent's is. Ah was born three doors by that in eighteen and eighty-three, an ah've lived in Donaghadee all ma life bar a short time ah was in Africa.' [This modest man visited Africa to fight for his country in the Boer War.]

'We moved from there to the Lane here, and we never lived any other place in Donaghadee. My father and mother and three sisters all died here, and my brothers went till America.'

'The Sanny Raw is Shore Street. Then there was the Bullock Row, where they fetched the cattle down. There were no other streets coming in from Newtownards [until] they made the New Road round that way – the landlord did – and they could come down there if they wanted. The Bullock Row was a place where there was thatched houses – the roofs was thatched, the most of them, and some of them was slated as far as I can remember them in my day. There was an old farmstead there where you go into Moat Avenue. A man called Jimmy Smith lived in it.'

'You know where Dorman's Isle is? Where the buses is? Before the railway was built, the tide washed right up to where the gasworks was [between William Street and Railway Street], right up to the big stores where they brought the corn in from Millisle. Then they called that Railway Street.'

'Then there was Saltworks Street. There was saltpans there, but I don't actually know where they were. And then the gas-works extended, and they took everything away.' [Telford's 1809 map shows Saltpan Bay to have been the small bay behind the South Pier. In the eighteenth century large iron pans were stood there, carefully set to catch sea-water at high tide. The hours before the next tide gave the salt-workers time to light large fires under the pans to boil off the water. The dry salt was then shovelled out before the next high water.]

'The coastguard station was round there where Neill's is [on the north-west corner of Manor Street and the Parade] – the Salvation Army Hall was the boathouse, and the chief officer [and other officers] stayed in a row of houses up an entry.'

'Of course the coastguards have went away now. They are not required. There is no more smuggling. No smuggling like what there was in the early days.'

The burn path. This quiet lane is centuries old. The once open burn was culverted for 'safety reasons' forty years ago.

'The lane they call Church Lane now, was called Mill Lane. The farmers all dumped their manure and seaweed at the foot of the Cannyreagh Road. All the farmers up that road when I was a boy, the Curraghs, the Keatings, the Carsons, the Carsons' forefathers, carted the wrack off the foreshore and emptied it there while the tide was out. And then when the tide was in they carted it up and put it on the fields.'

'The Killaughey Road was known as the Creighle Raw [out to the clay holes at Killaughey.] It never got going until they were going to get the airfield there [1944-45] and they started in and widened the road here and there.'[8]

'There was a public house at the corner of the New Street where McCaw's is now [the new Corner Shop]. It was The Auld House at Home. New Street mustn't have been very open at the time and it was narrow. I can remember them lowering New Street down [about three feet] – you can still see the steps up to a number of doorways.'

'Farmers would come [down New Street] with their carts, taking meal out of Jimmie Smith's – it was further down. Johnnie Sloan's was further down than that. And then there was Mary Eadie's and Captain Tosh's; they were tobacconists, and where the [Ulster] bank is were two or three old ladies, sisters, the Miss Caugheys, they had a very big house there, as big as the bank. They built the new bank in nineteen and twenty-two. I remember that anyway.'

'You've heard tell of the Murder Lane? They have changed the name of it [to Town Hall Lane]. The reason it got Murder Lane was when sailormen coming off a voyage went up to the public house that was at the head of it there – Grace Neill's bar.'

'Was anyone actually murdered in Murder Lane?' I ask.

'Well, you weren't murdered, but you were very near murdered. You know, you got a bloomin' good hidin' whenever you came from a public house and come down that way to get on the shore to go down to the harbour. I remember one or two gettin' a thumpin' up there, up that lane. But before that they said that people was murdered, but I don't know that there was ever anybody murdered in it, but "They got a good murderin," they'd have said.'

'Murder Lane' may be a reminder of the more ribald life of the eighteenth century port. Thankfully, for the present at least, things have somewhat calmed down.

11 Guns and grog

Grace Neill's

Just about every visitor to Donaghadee visits Grace Neill's in High Street. The inn's public bar is so redolent of 'the olden days' that one can easily people the place in one's mind with imaginary smugglers and revenue men, not to mention rebels from 1798. It is a joy not to be missed.

Grace Neill's is a very old hostelry. But when was it founded? The bar's signage states that it was established in 1611. But there is no evidence to support this claim, and as the most comprehensive study of the buildings of Donaghadee diplomatically puts it, this date is 'a little optimistic.'[1] It is unlikely that anyone would have built an inn this far outside of the necessary security of the tiny Scots pale just five short years after Montgomery's arrival.

It is also widely believed that no less a figure than Peter the Great stayed at Grace Neill's Inn.[2] And the records show that in 1698 the Czar of all the Russias did indeed come to the British Isles to learn how to build great warships, so that he might establish a Russian navy. But Peter's tight schedule left him no time for an Irish detour, much less a pint (or should that be a large vodka?) at Grace Neill's.[3]

However, they say there is no smoke without fire, and the myth of the visit of Peter the Great may have its origins in a real historical event. More than a century later, the Russian Archdukes Nicholas and Alexander arrived at Donaghadee on one of the packet boats.[4] However, there is no evidence that they visited the famous hostelry. It should also be pointed out that this visit took place in 1814 – four years before Grace Neill's birth, but romantics will never accept the dull truth.

Grace Neill, nee Jamieson, who was given the King's Arms when she married John Neill in c.1840. It is now universally known as 'Grace Neill's'. (Tom Neill Collection)

Grace Neill was born Grace Jamieson in 1817.[5] She married John Neill[6] and lived her whole life in Donaghadee, producing five sons, William, Tom, Alic, James and Hugh.[7] Grace was born into the bar trade. Her father Hugh gave her the King's Arms in High Street as a wedding present. After the early death of her husband in 1866, the vernacular name for these premises changed to 'Grace Neill's'.

In 1901, Grace is recorded as living in the same High Street bar with her only surviving son, James, who was landlord. By 1911, James had died, and the indefatigable Grace is recorded as landlady – not too shabby for a woman then in her ninety-fourth year![8] By repute, she was still serving customers until she died in 1916, leaving effects worth £434 10s 0d.[9]

Grace named her second child Thomas Tear Kelly Neill after a close relative, Thomas Tear Kelly MRCS, a surgeon who lived in Shore Street.[10] The surname Kelly, whilst common in Ireland, is relatively rare in north Down. But it often crops up in connection with the licensed trade in Donaghadee. In 1824,

Kelly's Steps and the former Downshire or Hillsborough Arms (centre), where Boswell stayed in 1769.

out of twenty licensed premises serving the small town, Robert Kelly owned an inn on High Street, and James Kelly had the Downshire Arms near the end of the Parade.[11] This is almost certainly the same tavern as was mentioned in 1818 by John Keats in another chapter. Indeed, it was also the Hillsborough Arms, where James Boswell stayed in 1769.[12]

These were the most prestigious of the Kellys' premises, and it is surely significant that the ancient steps opposite where this inn stood are still referred to as Kelly's Steps. For those arriving at the old harbour by sailing ship, these steps would have taken incoming passengers up to the customs-house. This was the first building passengers would have seen as they heaved their way to the top of the steps. The second would have been the Downshire or Hillsborough Arms.[13]

The old customs-house has gone and its remains lie buried under the roadway between Kelly's Steps and the fashionable frontage of Pier 36. The inn has remained, in a bright modern guise. Grace Neill's thrives too, dubious signage notwithstanding. I am sure Grace would have approved.

Heather Brown

Another slightly lesser-known name to conjure with is Heather Brown. Her story dates from 1905, with its terrible Old Year's Night storm. The last night of that year was a foul one. No-one ventured out except those with business that could not wait – the doctor, the telegraph linesmen, farmers, and of course lifeboatmen and coastguards.

At dusk, one of the coastguards at Ballywalter spied the *Catherine Renney* 'in front of a terrific wind with bare poles, the sails having been torn to shreds'. She wallowed in the huge waves, utterly helpless without her steering gear. The coastguards immediately put up a maroon. The Ballywalter lifeboatmen hooked four draught horses to a wagon carrying their boat and began to follow the rudderless vessel up the coast.

The *Catherine Renney* was a ninety-six ton sailing ketch out of Connah's Quay in north Wales. She had been built only four years earlier and was in good repair, but she was not equal to this storm. Soon she was off Coalpit Bay, just south of Donaghadee's Commons, desperately hoping that she could round the point and make the safety of the harbour.

However the fates were in an unforgiving mood, and at about six o'clock she struck the Brown Bull. This distinctive rock is visible at most states of the tide. As the waters recede it rises Poseidon-like, until at extreme low water it is

Sailing boats of the same type as the Catherine Renney.

The Brown Bull at its most benign. But with a high tide on a stormy night...

just reachable on foot. At six o'clock that evening it was just coming up to high-tide. Within minutes the residents of Princess Gardens and Shamrock Villas were called to the water's edge by heart-rending cries from the luckless *Catherine Renney*.

While the sea tore mercilessly at the stricken ship, there was pandemonium on shore. Men ran hither and thither through the Commons, and brought handcarts and wagons to see if they could help. Everyone knew what had to be done. A lifeline had to be got to the sinking vessel. But it was impossible to get a rope to the ship. She was too far out for throwing. Only a rocket could get a line to the *Catherine Renney*. Without one, there was little hope.

At eight o'clock the Ballywalter lifeboat-men arrived – with rockets. The sea was too bad for launching the lifeboat, but the rockets were fired over the

Renney's forecastle. The line was laid. Then the would-be rescuers saw a sight that chilled them to the marrow. The ship's crew had not the strength to tie off the lines, indeed they seemed to be so far gone that they had lost the very will to live. Their cries grew fainter, and slowly died away. Soon, no sign of life could be seen on the ship or in the water. That night four bodies were cast ashore. They were those of the ship's master and his three man crew.

With all the solemnity they could muster, the local people carried the bruised and broken bodies to Dawson's public house in New Street. Two days later, they were buried in a communal grave.[14]

The *Catherine Renney* had been carrying a cargo of inch-thick flags, about twelve inches square, of the sort used to pave kitchens and backyards. In the early weeks of the New Year these were gradually claimed by the sea as the wreck of the *Catherine Renney* was ground to pieces on the Brown Bull. Or so it was said. Miraculously, however, in those same weeks there was hardly a backyard in Donaghadee that did not suddenly get a facelift with a brand-new topcoat of quarry tiles.

Subject to modern-day salvage rules, anyone is welcome to gather such tiles

Time and tile wait for no man. Tiles from the wrecked Catherine Renney *graced many a yard in Donaghadee.*

Sir James Craig, the grandson of a Ballyvester man, supervised the gun running in 1914 and became Northern Ireland's first Prime Minister in 1921.

as they can carry from the Coalpit Bay foreshore and use them as they please. Before any readers rush off to gather a few, it should be pointed out that the depredations of the last hundred years have ensured that, although there are thousands of pavers still lying at the wreck site, none is larger than about three or four inches across. They are crazy-pavers now, easily recognised because they are almost exclusively triangular and look uncannily like soda farls, their colour always referred to as 'heather brown'.

The gun-runners of 1914

In the spring of 1914, while the rest of the world was worrying about war and rumours of war, Ireland was in the throes of the third Home Rule crisis. Edward Carson and James Craig led unionist opposition to Home Rule, vowing, in Randolph Churchill's words, that 'Ulster will fight, and Ulster will be right.' The authorities feared that the unionists might attempt to import arms. The Royal Navy patrolled the coast.

The government's fears were justified. Major Fred Crawford had already secured a large cache of guns and ammunition in Germany and Austria. By the end of March 1914, these were en route for Ulster. Near the Tuskar Rock, seven miles south-east of Rosslare Harbour, 216 tons of Mannlicher rifles and ammunition boxes were transferred to the *Clyde Valley*.[15]

On Saturday, April 25th the *Clyde Valley* steamed into Larne harbour before dawn and began unloading its boxes of rifles and bullets. After a fast and smooth operation, the ship crossed Belfast Lough to Bangor where an equally impressive decant was conducted.[16] As it did so, another small steamer, the *Innismurray*, appeared off the Great Copeland Island. The Donaghadee Harbour Master, Henry Collins, recorded that the ninety-four ton ship:

arrived and berthed about 5.45am today and landed what appeared to be packages and cases of arms. The Ulster Volunteers were here in great numbers.[17]

The Ulster Volunteer Force (UVF) had taken over the harbour. They had drilled on the Parade on Friday evening, then returned quietly in the small hours of Saturday morning. The telegraph lines were expertly shorted out. The town and port were sealed off. No policemen, coastguards or excisemen found near the harbour were allowed to leave; and those outside the town were not allowed to enter it. Every road was closed.

At 3.00am, the UVF commandeered the Neill Coal Company's crane on the pier. As soon as the *Innismurray* arrived (three hours late), boxes of rifles were

The scene on the south pier as the guns were landed. (PRONI)

immediately hoisted out of her hold. The unloading was done swiftly and efficiently. A queue of carts and lorries inched their way down the wall side of the south pier, turned a half-circle and took their turn beside the crane. It took less than two hours to unload seventy tons of weapons into the waiting vehicles. By 8.00am these had been dispersed all over Ulster, and the harbour once again bore the appearance of sleepy normality.

The UVF action had the tacit support of many of the officials who were on duty that night. Some of the policemen and coastguards who had been detained had pointedly turned their faces to the pier wall so that they could later state truthfully that they had seen nothing. The *County Down Spectator* felt similarly, describing the operation as 'a coup', 'an achievement,' and a job 'magnificently accomplished.' It also told the story of the night's only fatality.

Herbert Edward Painter was a thirty-eight year-old boatman in the coastguard service, and a man with a wife and two children. Ordered out to the station on the Warren Road on Friday evening by his officer-in-charge in Donaghadee, Painter had immediately jumped on his bicycle and ridden furiously along Shore Street. He never reached the coastguard buildings. At 1.00am, his lifeless body was discovered beside his bike just inside the station wall. Dr Nesbitt of Donaghadee pronounced Painter 'dead from heart failure due to over-exertion.'[18]

Later, when Sir Edward Carson was accused of not taking the death of the coastguard seriously, he made a statement to the *Times,* insisting that the death of Herbert Painter was not the fault of the UVF. However, he accepted that the man had died suddenly from heart disease, possibly accelerated by the excitements of the night, and suggested that some provision for the coastguard's family should be voted out of UVF funds.[19]

The imported arms were never used. But they did not need to be used to have political value, and possession alone gave the UVF important leverage. In August, the still-United Kingdom declared war on Germany. Most expected the Irish 'difficulty' to be shelved for the war's duration. On Easter Monday 1916, however, the followers of Patrick Pearse and James Connolly fired the shots that many had expected two years earlier.[20] The Easter Rising lasted only a week, but it led to partition, an Irish Free State and eventually an Irish Republic.

The quantity of munitions landed at Donaghadee was small compared to that landed at Larne and Bangor, and the Donaghadee landings are omitted from some versions of the story. What should not be forgotten is that it was at Donaghadee that the only fatality occurred. The night's operations were peacefully conducted, but one family at least will always remember the Donaghadee coastguard who lost his life because of them.

12 Tourist town

Suburbanisation

During the late nineteenth century, the town of Bangor expanded rapidly. This growth owed much to the railway, and to the B&CDR's shrewd exploitation of the desire of city-based businessmen to work in the metropolis and live in the more salubrious seaside air. The company sold good seaside housing at a fair price, offering purchasers first, second, or third class travel for ten years *for free,* an inducement many found difficult to resist.

Donaghadee's growth did not keep pace. The tortuous twenty-two-mile railway journey from Belfast to Donaghadee compared unfavourably with the twelve mile run from Queen's Quay to Bangor. The journey was also fifteen minutes longer and more expensive. Donaghadee found it hard to compete.

But there was growth all the same. The new century saw villas erected on New Road, Warren Road and Killaughey Road, all within walking distance of Donaghadee station. 'Gentlemen's terraces' convenient to the Millisle Road Halt appeared at Breeze Mount, Breeze Hill and Princess Gardens. Those who lived further afield could avail of bicycle parking spaces offered by Donaghadee businesses at a very reasonable penny a day.[1]

Mercifully, the green sward of the Commons was spared from development. But its old 'lazy beds', still visible today, ceased to yield their once familiar harvests of potatoes. Instead this wonderful stretch of green, which runs from the Quarry Hole to the High Robby, became available for recreation and leisure – even on a Sunday.

The old Georgian residences on Millisle Road's Barrack Hill experienced a more subtle but equally forceful assertion of Edwardian values. Rosebank

The Commons have changed from being a work place to a place of leisure, as these 'lazy beds', once used for growing potatoes, remind us.

Prospect House. Said to have changed hands for a shilling.

House remained aloof, but Ker's Villa became the Mount Royal Hotel; the decrepit old military barrack was swept away, and the fresh-water fish pond behind it was filled in.[2] In the barrack's place came Wesley Lodge, the former Methodist manse, which still stands at no. 7 Millisle Road.

One Georgian building that, fortunately, was not swept away is Prospect House, built opposite the foot of the Killaughey Road sometime before 1779.[3] It is said that one of its former owners decided that, instead of selling it, he would do better if he made it the grand prize in a raffle, charging a shilling a ticket. The tickets went like hot cakes. Eventually a lucky winner was given the title deeds to Prospect House, or as it was called by many – the Shilling House.

Summertime fun and frolics

By 1900, the ever-resourceful B&CDR was busy advertising the joys of holidays by the sea. Large numbers of visitors descended on the town every summer, and all sorts of attractions were developed to keep them entertained.

Regattas became commonplace in the harbour, and a golf club was established at the Warren. A Gentlemen's Bathing Place was built between 33 & 35A Warren Road. A Ladies' Bathing Place (now no. 29A), was also founded, but superseded in 1924 by a communal swimming pool, in which the bright young things of the Twenties overthrew tight-corseted Victorian morality.

Wealthy folk bought summer villas opposite the Copelands. Others bought fine homes in the General's Field on the Millisle Road, near both sea and railway. George Delacherois developed two cul-de-sacs there. He was persuaded by Donaghadee Urban District Council to call one of them Gloucester Avenue instead of his own choice of Marina Avenue, but insisted on naming the other The General's Walk after his great-uncle.[4] His daughters began to develop Leslie Hill, but soon handed over the work to a building firm.[5]

Naturally, not everyone who grew fond of Donaghadee wanted, or was able, to live there permanently. Between the wars, thousands of Belfast shipyard and mill-working families rented houses here for their fortnight's holidays.

For families used to a kitchen house without a garden, these houses were a treat. They served ten months every year as Donaghadee people's dwellings, but in July and August of each year, their residents vacated their homes and decamped to a 'back-house' at the rear of the property. Sometimes the backhouse was built of stone or brick, but often it was made of wood. The holiday rental money they gained was a useful addition to the family's income, and the presence of genial company made a welcome diversion during the summer months. The back-houses are now mostly gone, but the occasional one is still used as a storehouse or garage.

The most desirable time for a holiday in those days was during what was always known as 'the Twelfth week and the week after.' This July holiday was often extended to a month, with the man of the house taking the train to work for the extra fortnight, then returning to enjoy the delights of the seaside during the long summer evenings.

The people who came on these holidays remember endless, soporifically balmy days, with the healthy Donaghadee breeze kicking in during the evening to restore the spirit. Young children dreamed their days away as pirates or sea captains, firing broadsides of oar-splashes at each other along with volleys of laughter. They caught crabs with limpets knocked off the rocks; they dug up eelworms and luggies for deep-sea fishing later in the day, and went to the Commons for tennis or putting.

Older 'weans' girned for permission to go to Joyland, or join their parents for an ice-cream or a pastie supper in one of the establishments run by Italian

We have discovered a sweet little cove near here.

Some visitors had romance in mind. (Robert Neill Collection)

'Dare I wear this two-piece?' Many will have fond memories of Donaghadee's former swimming pool. (Robert Neill Collection)

Donaghadee became a favourite tourist destination, with all the fun and frolics that this entailed. (Robert Neill Collection)

families like the Capronis, Nardinis, Gregos and Giovannolis. Or perhaps they were dodging their parents for a few minutes, chasing each other for a stolen kiss.

Summer visitors flocked to the south pier to watch the Pierrots or the concert parties – until the rattling money-box came around, that is. The appeal of a few carefree weeks in an airy seaside town to families used to the grind of winter in the smoggy and noisy city is not to be underestimated. Many families visited every year.

In the period between the wars, many who had come to love the life by the sea pitched a caravan at Ballyvester or Millisle. Others bought a small patch of ground and built a wooden holiday home on it – all easily reached by the railway. Many of these wooden houses have now gone. Some have been replaced by grander dwellings, now often permanently occupied.

The 'Dee at war

When war was declared in September 1939, families with men at sea became concerned for their safety. In 2006 Betty Henry, née Lindsay, recalled how her family despaired to know if her father was safe. Along with his own dad, Betty's father had *twice* been torpedoed by U-boats in the First World War when they worked for the Head Line. By 1939 he was working on the Kelly coal-boats. This family needed no tuition on the danger to the sailors of the Merchant Navy. The 'Battle of the Atlantic' arrived on their doorstep when collier ships crossing the Irish Sea came under threat from German submarines.

Some young men and women joined the army, navy and air-force. Royal Engineers from Scotland were billeted in boarding-houses on Shore Street, and the Air-Sea Rescue Service commandeered the building now known as Ocean Drive. When the call to arms eventually reached the United States, their GIs came to Donaghadee too. Various foodstuffs, especially from overseas, became scarcer, and Ration Books were issued.

On four dark nights in April and May 1941 squadrons of Dorniers and Junkers punctured Belfast's inadequate defence of twenty-four heavy anti-aircraft guns, half-ready searchlights and no smokescreens.[6] They inflicted horrific blast-bomb and incendiary damage on the city.

Fire engines from as far away as Dublin rushed to aid the people of Belfast. This had unfortunate repercussions for the Irish Free State. When war had broken out, the German Foreign Minister, Joachim von Ribbentrop had informed Eamonn de Valera that Germany would respect his country's neutrality so long as they maintained it. But sending fire-engines and ambulances north was considered unacceptable. The bombing of the North Strand in Dublin some days later was as much a calculated warning to the Free State as the 'accident' that it was portrayed as.

The affair had an ironic resonance in Donaghadee. Many remembered the day, not too long before the War, when Lord Londonderry had hosted von Ribbentrop at Mount Stewart, and had brought him for a round of golf at Donaghadee. Some had even caddied for the visitors.[7]

As the Luftwaffe threat lessened, war at home settled into a routine that was on the one hand sombre, but on the other, buzzing with life. Dances were frequently held in Millisle and Donaghadee. Local girls found future husbands among the British and American servicemen. Many of these girls found rewarding war-effort employment in factories in Newtownards – some making parts for Stirling bombers.

Being beside the sea had an unforeseen bonus too. Local boatmen ferried small cargoes to and from huge transport ships in return for a few packets of

Donaghadee girls Jean Lock (nee Somers, left) and Mavis Warden (nee Tollerton, r) with American GIs Bob Leishman (left) and Frank Kouri (r) in April 1944. Private Kouri was killed during the D-Day landings two months later. (Jean & Ralph Lock)

tea, or a bag of sugar, or some other treat.

There is a persistent story that survived the news media reporting restrictions during the spring of 1944. At a time when beaches were being utilised for D-Day training, some observant locals were surprised to see two mature-looking men deep in discussion as they walked along Donaghadee's foreshore. The surprise was caused by their recognition of the well-known figures of Winston Churchill and General Dwight Eisenhower.

When V.E. Day eventually arrived the relief was almost overpowering. Street parties were arranged, and life gradually returned to normal. The air-raid shelters came down, the troops disappeared and slowly the range and amount of foodstuffs grew as imports could now arrive safely. The war had been a time of never-to-be-repeated horrors and fears – but the awfulness seemed to heighten awareness of the brevity of life, and this in turn created an atmosphere that had made for a giddy and exciting social whirl.[8]

The end of the line

After the Second World War, a series of unfortunate events conspired to bring about the end of the Belfast-Donaghadee railway. The economics of railway travel were already in doubt when, in 1945, a terrible rail crash near Ballymacarrett took the lives of twenty-two people, and with them most of the B&CDR's very limited contingency fund.

On October 1st 1948, after scarcely any public debate, it was announced that Northern Ireland's railways were to be nationalised. In early 1950, contrary to the wishes of most of their customers, the Northern Ireland Road Transport Board decided to close the railway lines from Belfast to Donaghadee and Newcastle. A few weeks later, on the suitably miserable, wet morning of April 24th 1950, the last train left Donaghadee.

Everyone wanted to say that they had been on the last train, so very seat was taken, even though many tickets were only valid for one stop. Driver Thomas Girvan, fireman James Clegg, and two men with almost eighty years' service between them, William Petticrew and Davis Saunders, bade their farewells to the Donaghadee Stationmaster, another forty-year-man called Alfred Jamison. At the Millisle Road Halt, hordes of passengers dismounted, and hordes more boarded for the next bit of the journey.

Mary Ann Miskimmon, who saw the first train come and the last train go. (Jean Cowan)

Many more found vantage points from which to witness the event. An elderly lady from Ballyvester, Mrs Mary Ann Miskimmon, stood on Semple's Bridge on the Killaughey Road. She had more reason to be there than most. In

Semple's bridge on Killaughey Road. What must Mrs Miskimmon's thoughts have been as she watched the last train leave?

1861, at the age of seven, she had watched the first train steam into Donaghadee, the only surviving person known to have done so. She had watched it come in from Logan's Arch at Herdstown, and she was determined to see the last one out.

The closure was intensely unpopular, but the new Ulster Transport Authority was determined that no amount of protest would reopen the lines. Over the subsequent weeks, with what many saw as an indecent haste, level crossings were destroyed and railway lines lifted. Only the bridges and embankments remain to remind us of the railway's former grandeur.

In 2002, there were 2,608 registered motor-cars in the town. What was the figure in 1950? One can hear the answer, 'Maybe a hundred' floating in the air. Those car-owners who journey to Belfast or other towns every day, and those who depend upon bus connections, have lived to deeply regret the short-sighted closure of its rail link.

But Donaghadee weathered the closure. Between 1901 and 2001 its population grew from 2,073 to 6,474.[9] It now serves Belfast, and places such as Bangor and Newtownards, as a dormitory town. Employers have come and gone. Easily the largest and most unforgettable of these was Cyril Lord, the self-made millionaire from Lancashire, who built a huge carpet factory on the Bangor High Road in 1957. It is a measure of Lord's ambition that, for a long time, this custom-built factory held the distinction of having 'the longest unbroken brick wall in Europe'.

The Karpet King's business brought much employment to the Donaghadee area, not to mention extra local spending power. Along with his other mills, hotels and restaurants, it also brought him hugely increased wealth. But quite suddenly, in 1968, his empire collapsed and he was forced to leave his fine home on the Warren Road and move to Barbados.[10] The factory rallied fitfully under a series of new owners, but declining sales and overseas competition forced its final closure in 2005. This was followed by its demolition. A sewage treatment plant is intended for the site.

In 1969, 'The Troubles' began. Thirty-five years of discontent and intermittent violence followed. During these, Donaghadee experienced at least two bomb attacks (mercifully without major casualties), and specific stresses such as the UWC strike, but all in all it suffered relatively lightly compared with other more divided parts of the Province. Today, just about everyone wants to believe that time has run out for those who would use violence to

Bollards to you too! During the 1970s, when fear of car bombs was at its height, bollards were laid along New Street to prevent parking near the courthouse (the former Market House).

achieve their ends. The vast majority recognises that it is time to negotiate a settlement that will be acceptable to all.

Donaghadee has been nothing if not adaptable over the years. It has taken blows, seized opportunities, and served as an occasional bit-part player in events of great moment. It has dutifully adjusted to the roles of seaside resort and dormitory town, while retaining much of its beauty and charm. But its fame has faded. The days when an Irish man or woman visiting London, or 'taking the waters' at Bath, could announce that they were travelling to Ireland through Donaghadee, and everyone in the cosmopolitan company would know the port they meant, are long gone.

Donaghadee is still very much a seaside town, and a desirable and pleasant place in which to live. Like a faded movie star, it is not quite what it was in its heyday, but most of the people who know and love it would have it no other way.

Townlands of Donaghadee parish, barony of Ards Lower

1   Ballybuttle
2   Ballycopeland
3   Ballycross
4   Ballydoonan
5   Ballyfrenis
6   Ballyhaskin
7   Ballyhay
8   Ballymacruise
9   Ballymoney
10 Ballynoe
11 Ballyrawer
12 Ballyrolly
13 Ballyvester
14 Ballywhiskin
15 Ballywilliam
16 Carney Hill
17 Carryreagh
18 Craigboy
19 Drumfad
20 Ganaway
21 Grangee
22 Herdstown
23 Hogstown
24 Islandhill
25 Kilbright
26 Killaughey
27 Millerhill
28 Sloanstown
29 Templepatrick
30 Townparks of
    Donaghadee

Notes

Chapter 1

1 *Regional geology of Northern Ireland,* p.20-21.
2 The name seems to refer to the coal-like appearance of the surrounding rock.
3 *Archaeological Survey of County Down,* p.11; *Portavo: an Irish townland and its peoples,* part I, p.40.
4 *Archaeological Survey of County Down,* p.65-68.
5 Ibid., p.57-58.
6 *Place-names of Northern Ireland,* vol.2, p.177-80.
7 *The Life of the Learned Sir Thomas Smith,* p.182.
8 *Ibid.,* p.27.
9 *Montgomery Manuscripts,* p.73.
10 Ibid. p.58.
11 www.apva.org
12 *The Montgomery Manuscripts,* p.61.
13 *Hibernica.*
14 *Montgomery Manuscripts,* p.61.
15 *Scottish Migration to Ulster,* p.246.
16 Rev. Andrew Stewart *His History,* p.61.
17 *Report on the customs in the northern ports of Ireland,* Charles Moncke, 1637.
18 *A History of Ulster,* p.122.
19 *Newtown,* p.57.
20 *Montgomery Manuscripts,* p.85, note 1.
21 *A History of Ulster,* p.123.
22 *Place-Names of Northern Ireland,* vol.2, p.177. The Montgomery family's title was supported by Letters Patent from the thirteenth year of the reign of Charles I. (Index of Delacherois and other Papers, PRONI, T/3179/4. This archive also contains the Letters Patent for the Manors of Newtown and Mount Alexander, Comber.)
23 *First Presbyterian Church, Donaghadee, 1642-1992,* p.6.
24 *Newtown,* p.56.
25 *The Scottish Migration to Ulster,* citing James I to Deputy Chichester, p.246.
26 *Ibid.,* p.248.
27 *Parliamentary Papers regarding Portpatrick and Donaghadee Harbours,* 1866, p.248.
28 *Calendar of State Papers relating to Ireland,* p.136-37.
29 *Two Centuries of Life in Down,* p.248.
30 www.royal-stuarts.org and www.canaan.demon.co.uk
31 Letters Patent from the court of Charles I, March 19th 1637. (PRONI, T/3179/4, T/3179/5.)
32 Lady Day, or the Feast of the Assumption of the Virgin Mary, fell on March 25th.
33 *Report on the customs in the northern ports of Ireland,* Charles Moncke, 1637, Donaghadee page. (PRONI, T/615/3, p.39-41.)
34 *Montgomery Manuscripts,* p.136. The stonework footings of this great building survive under the modern road surface. When the nineteenth century harbour works were proceeding, it was demolished to give access to the newer harbour's entrance.
35 Seventeenth century mail boats mail boats were sloop-rigged, i.e. single-masted and decked vessels of about sixty tons. Unpublished history of the Lemon family of Donaghadee, and Capt. R.H. Davis's notebook.
36 Donaghadee Muster Roll, 1642, (PRONI, T/3726/1).

Chapter 2

1 *The Irish Sword,* vol.VI, p.55. This typescript (dated 1963) is initialled *G de L,* presumably indicating George Delacherois.
2 *Kings in Conflict,* p.65.
3 *The Naval Side of King William's War,* p.259-60.
4 *Rooke's Account of Donaghadee Naval Affairs,* Hamilton Mss., Historical Manuscripts Commission, rep.II, app.6, 1887, p.186; Finch Mss., vol.II, 1922, p.233-35, 248-49.
5 www.ballyholmeuup.ukf.net
6 *The Antient and Present State of County Down,* p.129.
7 *Besieging and Taking of Carrickfergus,* in a letter from Chester, August 31st [1789]. (PRONI, D/1409/2).

8 *Kings in Conflict*, p.26 quoting source 49, a*n Impartial History of the Affairs of Ireland.*
9 Calendar of State Papers, Ireland, Bundle 402. The court proceedings were later sent to the Court of the King's Bench in Dublin.
10 The Clan Donald Archive, Sleat, Isle of Skye. (GD221333.)
11 Letter from Luke St. Lawrence, November 26th 1739, (GD221333.)
12 The trial documents imply that McMinn was the ship's owner, and as culpable as Davison, if not more so.
13 Gravestones inscribed with Hebridean names such as McKay and Morrison appear in a number of cemeteries in the Ards Peninsula. At least three that might very well be memorials to sons of the 'slaver's' passengers lie in Donaghadee Parish Graveyard.
14 Personal communication from Cailean MacClean, Skye historian, March 2004.
15 www.notolls.org.uk /skat/news80.htm, April 27th 1998.
16 Luke St. Lawrence to Alexander Cunningham, 1739, Clan Donald Archive. (GD221333.)

Chapter 3

1 www.bbc.co.uk/hist/war/plantation
2 *Portpatrick and Donaghadee Parliamentary Papers*, 1866.
3 Letter of July 20th 1776, Index of Delacherois and other Papers. (PRONI, T/3179/4, T/3179/5.)
4 *Leet's Directory,* unpaginated.
5 *Maps of the Roads of Ireland*. Examples of surviving posts may be seen at Frances Street, Newtownards, and Upper Newtownards Road, Dundonald.
6 *Two Centuries of Life in Down,* p.115, quoting a Thomas Montgomery letter of 1727 to his wife, Marie Angélique telling her that a Major Hamilton is doing just this as he writes.
7 James Hamilton, Earl of Abercorn, to Henry Mitchell Esq., 4th March 1748/49. (PRONI, D/623/A/13/34.)
8 *Belfast News Letter*, March 2nd 1962.
9 *Donaghadee Town Plan, 1859. (*PRONI, OS/9/43/1/1-9.)
10 *Men of the Ards*, p.102, 122, 139.
11 Richard Dill passport. (PRONI, T/2060/1.) Richard Dill (1786-1864) from Ballykelly in County Londonderry, went on to become a highly respected Presbyterian cleric.
12 John Keats's letters to Tom Keats, 3-9 July 1818, www.john-keats.com-letters. The inn can only have been the *Downshire Arms* kept by James Kelly in 1818.
13 *Belfast News Letter* (various) and *Newtownards Spectator,* 1936-40.
14 *Ibid.,* April 2nd 1802.
15 *Ibid.,* November 20th 1807.
16 *Ibid.,* November 20th 1810. 17 *Ibid.,* July 2nd 1811.
18 *Ibid.*, November 10th 1772.
19 Commissioners of Irish Lights, http://cil2.adnet.ie.
20 *Belfast News Letter*, November 22nd, & December 2nd 1791.
21 *More Extracts from the Naval Chronicle.* Letter from www.cronab.demon.co.uk/nch2htm.
22 The 'retired' ship was the mundanely named *Civil Service No. 5. (Newtownards Spectator*, February 15th 1941; article by John Moore of Donaghadee.)
23 Princess Victoria Papers, PRONI, D/3830/8/13. The *Sir Samuel Kelly's* crew on that day was:
Coxswain: Hugh Nelson, 2nd Coxwain: Alex Nelson, Motor Mechanic: Jim Armstrong, 2nd Mechanic: Sammy Nelson, Bowman: John Trimble, Crew-members: Hugh Nelson Junr., Frank Nelson, William Nelson, George Lindsay & Samuel Herron. John Trimble & Sammy Nelson were en route to Larne that day for the Donaghadee Towns' Cup rugby match, and missed the call.
24 Personal communication with the only living survivor, Hugh Nelson, July 2006 and http://news.bbc.co.uk /onthisday/hi/dates/stories/January/31/newsid.
25 Leach, p.211.

Chapter 4

1 *The Antient and Present State of County Down*, p.65.
2 *A Frenchman's Walk Through Ireland 1796-7*, p.225-26, 250-51.
3 *Boswell in Search of a Wife*, p.211-17.
4 Martin, *Life of James Boswell*, p.509.
5 Newtown Walk by Thomas Merry, and Donaghadee Walk by James Hunter, September 4th 1764. (Groves MSS, PRONI, T/808/15261.)
6 *Portavo*, part 1, various.
7 *Newtown*, various.
8 *Men of the Ards,* various.
9 Arbuckle to Robert Ross, January 1st 1797. (Downshire Papers, PRONI, D/607/E/1.)

10 William Hull to Lord Hillsborough, October 16th 1786. (Ibid.)

11 *Donaghadee Parish Register.*

12 *Pigot & Co's Directory of Ulster,* p.376-377.

13 Arbuckle to Hillsborough, December 27th 1786. (PRONI, D/607/E/1.)

14 *The Drennan-McTier Letters.* (PRONI)

15 *First valuation of Properties of Ireland,* p.71-81.

16 Mary Harding, the daughter of an A. Harding, Esq.

17 *The Drennan-McTier Letters.* (PRONI)

18 In 1796 Arbuckle complained to the Customs Board that, 'no Dublin paper arrives at this hamlet. It is a shame that government don't supply their collector with a newspaper favourable to monarchy and our blessed constitution.' Arbuckle to Ross, January 1st 1797. (PRONI, D/607/E/1.)

19 Arbuckle, Donaghadee, to Downshire, October 20th 1796. (Ibid.)

20 Ibid.

Chapter 5

1 Appendix no. II to the Report of the Secret Committee of the House of Lords, 1799. (Linen Hall Library, Belfast, N648 and Sheffield Papers, PRONI, T/3465/80.)

2 We can only wonder at what Arbuckle's thoughts must have been when he read in the *Belfast News Lette*r and the *Northern Star* that his old friend William Drennan had co-founded the United Irishmen.

3 *Men of the Ards,* p.263-303.

4 *British Parliamentary Papers, 1809 Report.*

5 Hull to Downshire, March 29th 1796. (PRONI, D/607/D/47.)

6 Hull to Downshire, October 30th 1797. (D/607/E/361.)

7 *British Parliamentary Papers, 1809 Report.*

8 Ibid.

9 *Belfast News Letter*, May 30th 1815.

10 *Papers Relating to the Mail Service to the North of Ireland,* no. 166, p.12, 1866.

11 *Belfast News Letter* August 4th 1821.

12 Logan had worked with Robert Stevenson on the Bell Rock lighthouse in 1807-10.

13 *Ordnance Survey Memoirs of Ireland,* vol.7, p.47.

14 *Belfast News Letter,* October 1st 1822, August 26th 1823, April 24th & 30th 1824.

15 *Belfast News Letter,* May 27th 1825.

16 www.bopcris.ac.uk/browse/eppiLCSH/34_2.html

17 *A Survey of British and Foreign Harbours,* vol.II, p.190.

18 http://cil2.adnet.ie

19 The original estimate for the harbour had been £145,453, but like many projects it overran, and finally cost £149,196. This elegant but functional arch would have included four-storey accommodation for a harbour-master.

Chapter 6

1 Batt to the Lords of the Treasury, *British Parliamentary Papers, 1823,* vol.vii, Appendix 15, p.151.

2 *Belfast News Letter,* May 6th 1825. With a favourable wind, the steam packets could manage about 8 knots, or about the same speed as a cutter, but at a heavy cost in coal.

3 Continuation of Parliamentary Paper, no.166, p.12, November 14th 1867.

4 *Belfast News Letter*, August 28th 1829.

5 *Ibid.*, January 28th 1803.

6 www.london-footnotes.co.uk

7 Reports to the Parliamentary Select Committee, January 29th 1823, (486) V.P. 291.

8 *Belfast News Letter,* October 13th 1829.

9 Cornell died near Brantford, Ontario in 1850, aged 53 years. His death is recorded on a stone in Donaghadee Parish Graveyard, but without reference to his short career as a diver. (*Gravestone Inscriptions*, vol.14, alphabetical entry.)

10 *Belfast News Letter*, June 24th 1834.

11 *Belfast News Letter* articles by Captain R.H. Davis.

12 *Dumfries Monthly Journal*, September, 1825.

13 *Belfast News Letter,* June 26th 1849.

14 British Parliamentary Papers, 1857, p.33-35.

15 These were John Jamieson, younger brother of Grace Neill, and some others from Donaghadee.

16 British Parliamentary Papers, (356), lxiii, 1867-68.

17 Letter from D.S. Ker, November 21st 1853. (PRONI, T/3179/4, T/3179/5.)

18 Daniel Delacherois had been obliged to raze his popular Sea Baths Hotel at the Saltpan Bay shore. He and his partner James Duffy used the compensation money to open the new Ulster Baths Hotel in 1872.

19 *Belfast News Letter,* June 24th 1861. The railway station premises now house the Meadowbank Social Club.
20 B&CDR minutes, 4th June 1861. (PRONI, UTA/20/A/4.)
21 *The Irish Builder,* no. 962, vol. XLI, February 15th 1900, p.273, & March 1, 1900, p.295.
22 In later life he was Sir Lynden Livingston Macassey, KBE, KC, MA, LLD, D.Sc. (1876-1963).
23 Directly between Donaghadee and Portpatrick is the 900 feet deep Beaufort Trench, famous today as the dumping ground for disused Second World War munitions. The maximum depth in the English Channel is about fifty metres.
24 Macassey believed that the tunnel would take up to forty years to dig.
25 *British and Irish Railway Tunnel Syndicate.* Drawing dated June 11th 1886, prospectus dated October 8th 1886. (PRONI, T/3179/4, T/3179/5.)

Chapter 7

1 *Ulster Dialects, An Introductory Symposium; www.HamiltonMontgomery1606.com,* p.7. In 1621 Sir William Alexander was given great tracts of land in what we now call Nova Scotia.
The brothers were the sons of a Captain Samuel de la Cherois who is believed to have lived in the small town of Cheroy near Sens in the Yonne region, and then at Ham on the River Somme. *The Huguenots and Ulster,* catalogue no.26.
2 *The Impact of the Domestic Linen Industry in Ulster,* p.68-69, 209.
3 *The Huguenots and Ulster,* note 2c. This publication lays bare the complex connections between the Crommelin and Delacherois families.
4 Some of the property's internal timbers have been ring dated to c.1640 by the present owners, Morris & Sylvia Reid.
5 This is the 'John Dillon' *Map of Donaghadee,* dated 1780 by Stevenson in *Two Centuries of Life in Down,* p.242-43. Mrs Georgina Stone informed the author some twenty years ago that she believed the map to be earlier, and that it perhaps even dated from c.1700.
6 There are surviving letters which predate his arrival headed 'The Manor House, Donaghadee'; and we know that James Boswell enjoyed tea and supper there in 1769. *Boswell in Search of a Wife,*

p.213.
7 *Buildings of North County Down,* p.85.
8 Plan of Donaghadee, dated '1780', reproduced in *Two Centuries of Life in Down,* p.250-51.
9 *The Huguenots and Ulster,* page after note 24.
10 Probably 1819, *Donaghadee and Portpatrick,* p.20.
11 *The Huguenots and Ulster, 1685-1985,* Delacherois Family Tree, page after cat. no.24.
12 *Ordnance Survey Memoirs of Ireland,* vol.7, Bangor, p.19-25; Donaghadee, p.45-53.
13 *Census of Ireland, 1871, Enumerator's Abstract,* p.240-50. The women's records are treated in the next chapter.
14 1859 Town Plan of Donaghadee. (PRONI, OS/9/43/1/1-9.) This shows that the Delacherois sea baths lay almost exactly on the site of the amenity area in Railway Street.
15 Dr Bill Crawford has long urged keen history students to produce a comprehensive picture of their town by using a Street Directory in conjunction with a contemporary town plan and a copy of the General Tenement Valuation – both of which are available at the PRONI.
16 *County Down Directory, 1886,* p.307-11.
17 This one-sided thoroughfare is also sometimes referred to as 'Cattle Loanin'.
18 Donaghadee had been equipped with domestic gas supplies since 1860.
19 *Newtownards Chronicle,* July 2nd 1904.
Donaghadee Parish Register. The ages of those who died are of a piece with the national figures. About a quarter were children, a quarter were young adults, a quarter middle-aged, and a quarter elderly; half were male, half female: no-one was immune. The register dates from 1771.
20 Donaghadee Urban District Council Copy Letter Book, 1. (PRONI)

Chapter 8

1 History of the Lemon family of Donaghadee; Capt. R.H. Davis's notebook. (PRONI, D/2015/5/5/7.)
2 *Belfast Street Directories 1840-50.*
3 *Ibid., 1845-64.*
4 First Donaghadee Presbyterian Church records show that Captain Tedford (the usual title for a ship-owner at that time) married

Margaret Lowry, and that they baptised five children there. They had to suffer the early loss of two children, but brought up two healthy sons, David and James, and a daughter, Elizabeth, all born between 1838-48.

5 *Ordnance Survey Memoirs of Ireland*, vol.7, p.48.

6 The tambour frame was similar to that of the tambourine.

7 *The Lagan Valley 1800-1850*, p.108.

8 *The Impact of the Domestic Linen Industry in Ulster*, p.50-55.

9 *Pigot's Directory of Ulster*, p.377.

10 *The Industries of Scotland*, p.307.

11 *Sewing and Social Structure: The Flowerers of Scotland and Ireland*, p.245.

12 *Slater's Commercial Directory of Ireland*, p.451.

13 *Belfast & Ulster Street Directory*, p.704-07. Jamison's factory was at 4 Shore Street.

14 *The Industries of Scotland, p. 310.*

15 *Ireland: its Scenery, Character, &c*, p. 85n.

16 *Northern Whig*, February 6th 1847.

17 *The Industries of Scotland*, p.308-09.

18 In 1871, by comparison, over a hundred townswomen of Donaghadee were recorded as 'wife', or as the mistress of a boarding house, seventy were domestic servants and eleven were shopkeepers. *Census of Ireland for the year 1871.*

Chapter 9

1 www.historyfromheadstones.com

2 *Donaghadee and Portpatrick* p.9. Arrow loops are visible on the exterior, and substantial fireplaces in the interior of the first floor of the tower.

3 *Ordnance Survey Memoirs of Ireland*, vol.7, p.48.

4 Of the twenty-four Presbyterian ministers who served the Ulster colony between 1613-41, twenty were Scots, half of whom came from Ayrshire. *Fasti of the Irish Presbyterian Church,* p.3-15.

5 John Scott, quoted in *Two Centuries of Life in Down*, p.350.

6 *First Presbyterian Church, Donaghadee, 1642-1992.*

7 Thirty inch Town Plan of Donaghadee, 1834, T/2933/4/217.

8 Newtown and Donaghadee Walk, 1784. (Groves MSS, PRONI, T/808/15261.)

9 *Fasti of the Irish Presbyterian Church*, p.231.

10 First Property Valuation. (PRONI, VAL/1B/32.)

11 Plaques in the church: *Ordnance Survey Memoirs of Ireland,* *vol.7*, p.45-51.

12 In 1849, Skelly was succeeded at Shore Street by his son, the Rev.William Finlay McEwen Skelly.

13 *Ordnance Survey Memoirs of Ireland,* vol.7, p.45-51.

14 The present 'Town Hall' was built as a private house in the late eighteenth century, and soon afterwards became a hotel.

15 Tradition has it that the corn-mill stood where John Bennett had his yard.

16 Index of Delacherois Papers. (PRONI, T/3179/5.)

17 Donaghadee Methodist Mens' Club, pers. comm.

18 *The Methodist Church, Donaghadee 1790-1959; Donaghadee and Portpatrick*, p.14.

19 *Donaghadee Graveyard.*

20 It contains the remains of many people named in this work, such as Rev. Andrew Stewart, James Lemon, James Tedford and Grace Neill.

21 Jean Mackgwear's headstone is assumed by many to be Donaghadee's oldest recorded grave, but in the old style Julian calendar, the end of the year was Lady Day (or the Feast of the Assumption of the Virgin Mary) on March 25th. This puts William Scott's date of death roughly forty days earlier than the Mackgwear date.

22 *The London Gazette*, September 7th, 1920.

It occupied what by the 1960s had become a tired old building, built as a Masonic Hall at the beginning of the nineteenth century, then used as a school. For a few years before it was demolished, it served as a Sea Scout Hall.

23 Index of Delacherois Papers. (PRONI, T/3179/5.) Rear-Admiral Leslie had entered the Royal Navy in 1793. After a forty-year career as an officer in the Royal Navy he died in 1851.

24 Applications for Grant Aid for National Schools: PRONI, ED1/15, and MIC/548/31-36.

25 Found in a manuscript notebook that came from papers donated by J.P. Corry. This collection is held at PRONI, and currently cannot be found. Fortunately for our story, the author transcribed its contents, and a typescript is held by the Principal of Ballyvester Primary School. Corry bought the nearby Rathmore House (Croagh Patrick) in Ballyvester, a century ago.

Chapter 10

1 *Archaeology of Ulster*, p.109.

2 Ordnance Survey Memoirs, Manuscript Field Name Book for Parish of Donaghadee, unpaginated. (PRONI, MIC/6A/30.)

3 Andrew Ringland's forge was where Donaghadee's Free Presbyterian Church now stands.

4 The mill building later served as a fire station, a motor repair garage and a builder's stores.

5 Bill of Charges for the Manor Pound of Donaghadee otherwise Montgomerie, Act of 14th & 15th Victoria (1851-52), ch.92, dated July 1st 1858. (Delacherois Papers, PRONI, T/3179/5.)

6 As recently as the 1980s, the heavy slate slab with its carved gratings could still be found. A child, or a nosy historian, could get down on his knees and watch the water flow beneath it.

7 Cassette tape recording of John Bennett with some pupils of Donaghadee High School, 1974.

8 One wonders how many bricks in old Donaghadee houses were made of Killaughey clay, or with clay from the grassed over claypits just below the 2nd & 15th greens at Donaghadee Golf Club.

Chapter 11

1 *Donaghadee and Portpatrick,* p.15.

2 In some versions of the story he came to visit a shipyard at Warrenpoint. If he had, he would have been somewhat disappointed. Until the Hall family built a town on their rabbit warren in the eighteenth century, Warrenpoint consisted of only two houses 'and a few huts for the occasional residence of fishermen during the oyster season.' *Topographical Dictionary of Ireland; Parliamentary Gazetteer of Ireland,* p.473.

3 *Did Peter the Great Visit Ireland,* p.348-49.

4 *British Parliamentary Papers, 1858, p.18,* Admiralty Secretary, James Vetch, June 18th 1858.

5 She had two brothers, John, born in 1819, and Hugh John, born the following year. Donaghadee Parish Church Register, 1818-19.

6 The marriage is not recorded in the Donaghadee Register.

7 Gravestone inscription in Donaghadee Parish Graveyard.

8 1901 & 1911 Censuses of Ireland. (PRONI, MIC/354/3/69)

9 1916 Wills Calendar.

10 Much of the Neill family information supplemented by a personal communication from Grace Neill's great, great grandson, Dr. Thomas Kelly Neill, 2004.

11 *Pigot's Provincial Directory,* 1824, p.377.

12 On the death of his father the Earl of Hillsborough became the Marquis of Downshire.

13 On the bottom step there is an engraved V in the rock, probably to indicate how much draught there is for a boat at high water.

14 *The County Down Spectator and Ulster Standard,* January 5th 1906.

15 Gunrunning in Ulster, www.ollar.utvinternet.com/on/htm

16 *A History of Ulster,* p.444.

17 Ministry of Commerce file. (PRONI)

18 *County Down Spectator,* May 1st 1914.

19 www.coastguardsofyesteryear.org, quoting from the *Times,* April 28th 1914.

20 www.ollar.utvinternet.com/on/htm

Chapter 12

1 'The Auld Hoose at Home' at the top of New Street in Donaghadee was one of these.

2 Donaghadee Town Plan, 1859. (PRONI, OS/9/43/1/1-9.) It was where the school grounds of St. Anne's are marshy and full of rushes on both sides of the driveway.

3 *Historic Buildings in Donaghadee and Portpatrick,* p.30.

4 Brigadier-General George Francis Leslie of Mount Royal.

5 Personal communication from Mrs G.M. Stone, Feb 7th 1994.

6 www.historyireland.com, and www.ww2.com

7 Personal communication from Maurice Bunting.

8 Much of this wartime information came from Betty Henry, who lived through the war.

9 Northern Ireland Census Office.

10 *Irish Times* June 5th 1984, p.5; *Belfast Telegraph,* May 30th 1978, p.8

Bibliography

Books & periodicals
Adams, Brendan *Ulster Dialects: An Introductory Symposium* (Holywood, 1964)
Agnew, Jean, (ed.) *The Drennan-McTier Letters, 1776-1793* (Dublin, 1993)
Allen, Harry *The Men of the Ards* (Donaghadee, 2004)
Bardon, Jonathan *A History of Ulster* (Belfast, 1992)
Bassett, George Henry *County Down Directory, 1886* (Dublin, 1886)
Belfast and Ulster Street Directories (Dublin, 1852, 1863-64)
Boswell, James *Boswell in Search of a Wife* (London, 1769)
Boyle, Elizabeth *The Irish Flowerers* (Belfast, 1971)
Bremner, David *The Industries of Scotland, their Rise, Progress and Present Condition* (Glasgow, 1869)
Brett, C.E.B. *Buildings of North County Down* (Belfast, 2002)
Burke, Sir Bernard *Burke's Landed Gentry in Ireland* (London, 1904)
Carr, Peter *Portavo, an Irish townland and its peoples, part one* (Dundonald, 2003); *part two* (Dundonald, 2005); *The Most Unpretending of Places: A History of Dundonald, County Down* (Dundonald, 1987)
Clarke, Richard *Gravestone Inscriptions, vol.14, Donaghadee & Templepatrick Graveyards* (Belfast, 1974)
Collins, Brenda 'Sewing & Social Structure: the flowerers of Scotland and Ireland' in Mitchison, R., and Roebuck, Peter *Economy and Society in Scotland and Ireland, 1500-1939* (Edinburgh, 1988)
Collins, Brenda, Philip Ollerenshaw & Trevor Parkhill, (eds.) *Industry, Trade and People in Ireland 1650-1950, essays in honour of W.H. Crawford* (Belfast, 2005)
Crawford, William H. *The Impact of the Domestic Linen Industry in Ulster* (Belfast, 2005)
Davis, Captain R.H. *Deep Diving and Submarine Operations, 8th edition* (Cwmbran, Gwent, 1981)
Day, Angélique and McWilliams, Patrick, (eds.) *Ordnance Survey Memoirs of*

Ireland, Parishes of County Down II, 1832-4, 1837, vol.7 (Belfast, 1991)
De Bougrenet, Jacques Louis, Chevalier de la Tocnaye *A Frenchman's Walk Through Ireland 1796-7* (Cork, 1798; Belfast, 1984)
Dickson, Hugh (with Kenneth Kenmuir) *Historic Buildings in Donaghadee and Portpatrick* (Belfast, 1977)
Doherty, Richard *The Williamite War in Ireland, 1688-1691* (Dublin, 1998)
Eagleson, Rev. George McK, and Tom Johnston *First Presbyterian Church, Donaghadee, 1642-1992, A Historical Review* (Newtownards, 1992)
Green, E.R.R. *The Lagan Valley, 1800-1850* (London, 1949)
Hall, Mr & Mrs S.C. *Ireland, its Scenery, Character Etc.* (London, 1891)
Harris, Walter *The Antient and Present State of County Down* (Dublin, 1744); *Hibernica, Or some Antient Pieces relating to Ireland, Part 1* (Dublin, 1747)
Hill, G., (ed.) *The Montgomery Manuscripts* (Belfast, 1869)
Hodges, H.W.M. *Ulster Journal of Archaeology, 3rd series, vol.18* 'The Excavation of a Group of Cooking Places at Ballycroghan, County Down' (Belfast, 1955)
Hughes, A.J., and Hannan, R.J. *Place-Names of Northern Ireland, vol.2, Co. Down II, The Ards* (Belfast, 1992)
Irish Builder no.962, vol.XLI (Dublin, Feb.15th 1900)
Irish Provincial Directory (London, 1824)
Irish Sword, vol.VI (Dublin, 1963)
Jope, E.M. and Wilson, B.C.S. *The Ulster Journal of Archaeology, vols.19 & 20* 'A Burial Group of the First century A.D. near Donaghadee, County Down' (Belfast, 1956 & 1957)
Leach, Nicholas *For Those in Peril* (Kettering, 1999)
Leet's Directory to the Market Towns, Villages and Gentlemen's Seats and other, Noted Places in Ireland (Dublin, 1814)
Leet's List of Post Towns in Scotland (Dublin, 1814)
Lewis, Samuel *Topographical Dictionary of Ireland, a Historical and Statistical Description* (London, 1837)
McCavery, Trevor *Newtown: A History of Newtownards* (Dundonald, 1994)
Maguire, W.A., (ed.) *The Huguenots and Ulster, 1685-1985* (Belfast, 1985); *Kings in Conflict, Ireland in the 1690s* (Belfast, 1990)
Martin, Peter *A Life of James Boswell* (London, 1999)
The Methodist Church, Donaghadee, 1790 -1959 (Donaghadee, 1959)
Milligan, Saeton F. *Journal of the Royal Society of Antiquaries of Ireland* (Dublin, 1907)
Naval Chronicle Extracts 'Donaghadee, December 21st 1812'
Ordnance Survey Memoirs, Field Name Book for Parish of Donaghadee (Dublin, 1835)
Parkhill, Trevor and Speers, Sheela (eds.) *Kings in Conflict, Ireland in the 1690s* (Belfast, 1990)

Parliamentary Gazetteer of Ireland vol.III, p.473 (Dublin,1846)

Paul, Rev. F.J. and Stewart, Rev. David *Fasti of the Irish Presbyterian Church* (Belfast, 1937)

Perceval-Maxwell, M. *Scottish Migration to Ulster in the Reign of James I* (London, 1973)

Powley, Edward B. *The Naval Side of King William's War* (London, 1972)

Rennie, Sir John, C.E. *A Survey of British and Foreign Harbours* (London, 1838)

Robinson, Philip *The Plantation of Ulster* (Dublin & Belfast, 1984)

Roulston, William *History from Headstones* (Belfast, 2004)

Seward, Wm. Wenman *Topographia Hibernica* (Dublin, 1795)

Slater's Provincial Directory of Ulster (Dublin, 1846)

Smith, George, (ed.) *Dictionary of National Biography* (Oxford, 1921-22)

Stevenson, John *Two Centuries of Life in Down, 1600-1800* (Belfast, 1920; Dundonald, 1990)

Story, George *A True and Impartial History of the wars in Ireland* (London, 1691)

Strype, John *The Life of the Learned Sir Thomas Smith, Knight* (London, 1698)

Taylor and Skinner *Maps of the Roads of Ireland* (London & Dublin, 1778)

Wheeler, Marcus 'Did Peter the Great Visit Ireland?' *Irish Slavonic Studies, no.5, 1984; Pyotr I – materially diya biografii,* p.348-9, M.M. Bogoslovsky (Moscow, 1941)

Government reports and minutes

Census of Ireland Abstracts, 1852, Enumerators' Abstracts, Town of Donaghadee.

Census of Ireland for the year 1871, Occupations of Females.

1901 & 1911 Censuses of Ireland, Household and Building Returns.

General Tenement Valuation of Ireland, Dublin, c.1862.

Moncke, Charles, *Report on the customs in the northern ports of Ireland,* 1637, (PRONI T/615/3).

Minutes and Correspondence regarding Portpatrick and Donaghadee Harbours, 1866, (166/263) *vol.66, p.125-65,* deponent Captain Hawes, R.N.

Report of Select Committee studying Communication between England and Ireland by way of the north-west of Scotland, British Parliamentary Papers (394) vol.51 and (269) vol.3I, app.B, p.657 (HMSO, 1809)

Estimate of sums required in 1821 to defray expenses at Donaghadee and Portpatrick Harbours, Paper (556), vol.16, p.55 on (HMSO, 1821); *Paper (191), vol.18, p.385 on* (HMSO, 1822)

Further Estimate of Miscellaneous Services for the year 1823, British Parliamentary Papers, vol.3 (HMSO, 1823)

Appendix No. 15 to the Report from the Select Committee on Glasgow and Port-Patrick Roads. For the Establishment of Steam Packets between Portpatrick and Donaghadee, Paper (486), vol.5, p.133 on, British Parliamentary Papers, 1823;

Paper 428, vol.7, p.151 on, British Parliamentary Papers, 1824.
A Memorial of the Belfast and County Down Railway Company and landed Proprietors and Merchants (almost exclusively Irish), sent to parliament January 10th 1856 with almost 1000 signatures, *British Parliamentary Papers, 1857.*
Report on Donaghadee and Portpatrick Harbours, p.18, British Parliamentary Papers; Captain Vetch's Report to the Admiralty upon the Resumption of a Mail Packet Service, June 18th 1858.
Papers Relating to the Mail Service to the North of Ireland, via Portpatrick and Donaghadee Harbours, British Parliamentary Papers, Paper 166, p.12, 1866.
Letter from Lord Stair, Chairman of the Portpatrick Railway Company to the Secretary of the Treasury, Minutes and Correspondence relating to Portpatrick and Donaghadee Harbours, *British Parliamentary Papers, (356), vol.63, 1867-68.*

Newspapers
Belfast News Letter, County Down Spectator, Dumfries Monthly Journal, London Gazette, Newtownards Chronicle, Newtownards Spectator.

On-line sources
http:g.//bachelier.free.fr/lacharlonnie.htm;
http://cil2.adnet.ie;
http://en.wikipedia.org;
http://news.bbc.co.uk /onthisday/hi/dates/stories/January/31/;
www.apva.org /hist/;
www.bbc.co.uk/history/timelines/ni/schomberg/shtml;
www.bbc.co.uk /hist/war/plantation;
www.ballyholmeuup.ukf.net/groomsport.htm;
www.bopcris.ac.uk/browse/eppiLCSH/34_2.html;
www.blupete.com/hist/NovaScotiaBk1/Part1/Ch6;
www.cil.ie./flatareaEQLlighthousesAMPLighthouseIDEQL52.entry.html;
www.coastguardsofyesteryear.org;
www.cronab.demon.co.uk/nch2htm;
www.historyfromheadstones.com;
www.john-keats.com-letters;
www.macleodgenealogy.org;
www.nitakeacloserlook.gov.uk;
www.notolls.org.uk/skat/news80.htm;
www.ollar.utvinternet.com/on/htm;
www.royal-stuarts.org;
www.tartans.com/articles/famscots/boswellj.html;
www.HamiltonMontgomery1606.com; *The Montgomery Manuscripts: Hamilton & Montgomery, 400 Years, 1606-2006* (PDF e-book, Belfast, 2006).

Papers held by the Public Record Office of Northern Ireland (PRONI)
Abercorn Papers: D/623/A/13/34, D/623/A/25/22&50. **Downshire Papers:** Hull
to Hillsborough, October 16th 1786 (D/607/B/205); Arbuckle to Hillsborough,
December 27th 1786 (D/607/B/215); Hull to Downshire, March 29th 1796
(D/607/D/47); Arbuckle to Downshire, October 18th 1796, (D/607/D/240);
Arbuckle to Downshire, October 20th 1796, (D/607/D/243); Arbuckle to Robert
Ross, January 1st 1797, (D/607/E/1); Hull to Downshire, October 30th 1797,
(D/607/E/361). **Dufferin and Ava Papers:** D.S. Ker to Dufferin, January 10th
1859, (MIC 22, reel 3, vol.X). **Delacherois Papers**: *Bill of Charges for the Manor
Pound of Donaghadee otherwise Montgomerie,* dated 1858, (T/3179/5); Family
Papers, T/3179/4, T/3179/5 and MIC/321/6. **B&CDR Minute Book** UTA/20/A/4.
Education Papers: Applications for Grant Aid for National Schools, (ED1/15 &
MIC/548/31-36); *Inspectors' Reports*, (ED6 various). **Plans and property:** *30 inch
Town Plan of Donaghadee, with Valuations,* 1834, (VAL/1D/3/16); *First Valuation
of Properties*, 1834, (VAL/1B/32.); *Donaghadee Town Plan, 1859,* (OS/9/43/1/1-
9); *Valuation of Property Revisions,* (VAL/12B/23/13A-E). **Rev. Canon
Rutherford's Papers:** *Besieging and Taking of Carrickfergus, a Full and True
Account of the Duke of Schomberg,* (D/1409/2). **Calendar of State Papers relating
to Ireland**, 1615-25, T/827/1. **Capt. R.H. Davis's notebook:** D/2015/5/7.
Donaghadee Muster Roll, 1642, (T/3726/1). **Donaghadee Parish Register:**
(MIC/583/5 and CR1/54/2). **Irish State Papers:** T/448/1. **Lemon family papers**
(Donaghadee), an unpublished history, (T/1781/1). **Ministry of Commerce file**:
COM/9/18. **Newtown Walk** by Thomas Merry & **Donaghadee Walk** by James
Hunter, September 4th 1764, (T/808/15261). **Princess Victoria Papers:**
D/3830/8/13. **1916 Wills Calendar**.

Additional
National Archives of Ireland: Rooke's Account of Donaghadee Naval Affairs,
Hamilton Mss., Historical Manuscripts Commission, rep.2, app.6, 1887, p.186;
Finch Mss., vol.2, 1922, p.233-35, 248-49. **Clan Donald Archive:** (Sleat, Isle of
Skye), St. Lawrence to Cunningham, November 26th 1739, GD221333. **Salisbury
Manuscripts, British Museum:** Davies, Sir John, to the Earl of Salisbury, August
24th 1609, 127, folio 134. **Donaghadee Urban District Council Letters Book.**

Index